ADVANCE PRAISE

"*Amplify* will help you see warning signs of distress in your career and your life. It's an insightful approach to taking control and successfully traversing through midlife career challenges so you evolve and grow, doing what you love."

—BILL BORELLE, SVP, MARKETING, PITNEY BOWES

"With authentic narrative, practical models, and personal experience, Peter provides a compass for navigating the choppy waters of modern career and life issues."

—BOB WIELGOS, EXECUTIVE DEVELOPMENT, UNITED AIRLINES

"Drawing from his experience as a successful executive coach, Diamond brings a fresh perspective on the importance of having vision, values, and purpose."

—RENETTA MCCANN, EXECUTIVE COACH

PETER C. DIAMOND

AMPLIFY
YOUR CAREER AND LIFE

4 STEPS TO EVALUATE, ASSESS
and MOVE FORWARD

RIVER GROVE
BOOKS

Neither the publisher nor the author is engaged in rendering professional advice or services to the individual reader. The discussion or mention of any ideas, procedures, activities, product and suggestions in this book is not intended as a substitute for consulting with your physician, therapist, or other qualified professional and obtaining competent medical or professional advice and care as to any condition, situation, activity, procedure or suggestion that might affect your health or well-being. Each individual reader must assume responsibility for his or her own actions, safety and health. In short, this book and its contents are provided as-is with no representation or warranty of any kind. Neither the author nor the publisher shall be liable or responsible for any loss, injury or damage resulting from the reader's use, application, implementation or imitation of any information or suggestion in this book.

While the examples and case studies in this book are drawn from real client engagements, the names and identifying details or person mentioned have been changed or omitted to protect their privacy.

Published by River Grove Books
Austin, TX
www.rivergrovebooks.com

Distributed by River Grove Books

For ordering information or special discounts for bulk purchases, please contact River Grove Books at PO Box 91869, Austin, TX 78709, 512.891.6100.

Design and composition by Greenleaf Book Group
Cover design by Greenleaf Book Group

Publisher's Cataloging-In-Publication Data
Diamond, Peter C.
    Amplify your career and life : 4 steps to evaluate, assess and move forward / Peter C. Diamond.—First edition.
        pages : illustrations ; cm
    Issued also as an ebook.
    Includes bibliographical references.
    ISBN: 978-1-63299-007-5
    1. Self-actualization (Psychology) 2. Vocational guidance. 3. Change (Psychology) 4. Middle age—Psychological aspects. I. Title.
    BF637.S4 D53 2014
    158.1   2014945271

eBook ISBN: 978-1-63299-008-2

First Edition

Be forewarned. I do not believe that
getting older means getting old.

I embrace the notion that
we can change our lives.

We should be who we are
and live the life we want.

For some, this is a radical way of thinking.

For me, it was a radical way of being.

Once I took the plunge, I was able to activate
a more fulfilling and satisfying life.

You will too.

This book is dedicated to my father and brother.
Their shortened lives are a daily reminder of the importance of
living a thriving life today and going after what you want.

CONTENTS

ACKNOWLEDGMENTS xi

INTRODUCTION 1

STEP 1—INTERROGATING YOUR LIFE 7

CHAPTER ONE » FACING THE HARD TRUTH 9

My Story 9

CHAPTER TWO » WHAT IS THE ARC OF YOUR LIFE? 21

Life as a Free Agent: Our Twenties 22

I Want More: Our Thirties 24

Fraying at the Edges: Our Forties 27

Exercise: Your Life Arc 28

Career in Flux: Is This It? 28

Key Questions 31

CHAPTER THREE » ARE YOU FEELING BOXED IN? 33

The Seven W.A.R.N.I.N.G. Signs of Distress 38

What the Seven W.A.R.N.I.N.G. Signs Have in Common 49

What Is the State of Your Life? 52

The Life Line Assessment 55

Key Questions 61

It's Never Too Late to Reinvent Your Career 61

**STEP 2—FORMULATING YOUR PLAN TO
AMPLIFY YOUR LIFE** 63

CHAPTER FOUR » WHAT'S YOUR REALITY? 65

What Does It Mean to Move Forward? 70

Developing Your Dynamic Goals 72

Creating Space to Achieve Your Goals 77

Opening Up to Change 79
Put a Stake in the Ground 81
Being Ruthless with Your Time 82
I Want a Balanced Life!!! 83
Key Questions 86

CHAPTER FIVE » A REASON TO BELIEVE 87
Create Your Own Core Belief System 88
The Relevance of a Vision 90
How to Craft Your Vision 94
The Value of Values 95
How to Craft Your Values 98
The Pertinence of a Purpose 101
How to Craft Your Purpose 104
You and Your Core Belief System 105
Key Questions 107

STEP 3—CONQUERING OLD FOES 109

CHAPTER SIX » WHAT DOES SUCCESS LOOK LIKE? 111
Simon Has Restored His Confidence 111
Ethan Is No Longer at Sea 112
Miguel Has Regained His Identity 113
Marina Is Back in Control 115
Danielle Is No Longer Idling 115
Anna Has Her Focus Back 116
Patrick Feels Fulfilled 117
Uncovering Universal Themes 119
Key Questions 131

CHAPTER SEVEN » TAKE BACK YOUR LIFE. CONQUER OLD FOES. . . . 133
Your Saboteurs (Friend or Foe) 135
It Is About You 139
Reset Your Health: A Healthy Mind Needs a Healthy Body 140
Fits and Starts 146
Are You Suffering from Pre-Worrying? 147
Anticipate Happiness 149
Key Questions 152

CONTENTS

STEP 4—ADOPTING THE CHANGES YOU DESIRE 153

CHAPTER EIGHT » REALIZING THE LIFE YOU WANT. 155

A Desire to Thrive. 155

Seven Steps to Move You Forward 158

Five Patterns of Behavior That May Thwart Your Plan 159

Effort Leads to Engagement 165

When to Practice Patience 168

Key Questions. 174

CHAPTER NINE » AMPLIFIERS: THIRTEEN THRIVING TIPS. 175

1 Manage Your Emotional Energy 175

2 Get Moving. 177

3 Lighten Your Load 179

4 Watch Your Time 181

5 Take One Thing at a Time 183

6 Consider the Company You Keep 185

7 Be Kind 187

8 Meditate Nightly 189

9 Take Control of Your Spending Habits 190

10 Employ Energy Motivators. 192

11 Walk with Your Head Up and Your Eyes Open 193

12 Up Your Charismatic Quotient 195

13 Get Out of That Rut. 196

Key Questions 198

PARTING WORDS 199

NOTES 203

FURTHER READING 205

ABOUT THE AUTHOR 207

READING GROUP GUIDE 209

ACKNOWLEDGMENTS

When I decided to write this book, I stepped far outside my comfort zone. In my heart, I knew it was aligned with my core belief system but in my head my saboteurs were running rampant. I soldiered on slowly and alone in the beginning. Knowing that this undertaking was beyond my current skill set, I elicited help from my first editor and writing coach, Delia Coleman. She helped me shape the outline and refine the initial three chapters, setting the tone for the rest of the book. With a preliminary draft in hand, I enlisted the help of a manuscript doctor, Vicki Gibbs, who saw the potential and challenged me to create a structure that has become the four steps. The third and most inspiring source of help was Katherine Pickett. Her unfailing support and belief in the message gave me the confidence to persevere. A true partner, she coached me and fortified me to be a better writer. What I admire the most about Katherine is that she is a "we" user. All of her comments were "we should . . . " This immediately signaled to me that she was invested in this project. I was no longer alone in what is a lonely process.

My heartfelt appreciation goes out to Amy Kleckner, Judith Cohen, Jeanie Caggiano, Lisa Zarick, Ryan VanMeter, Kate Cicchelli, Liz Cicchelli, Sarah Butterfield, Sara Abu-Rumman, Stephanie Thompson, Ann Angel, and Kelly Byer my beta readers and book group who willingly provided feedback and insights to strengthen the manuscript and emboldened me to see it through to publication. To the incredible team at River Grove Press, Hobbs Allen, Lindsey Clark, Brian Phillips, Chelsea Richards, Carrie Jones, Sally Garland, and Carly Cohen, thank you for being patient and shepherding me through the unnerving process of publishing my first book. Jessica Cella, your keen eye and attention to detail brought clarity and simplicity to the workbook. To Smith Publicity for helping me launch the book and myself with aplomb. Finally, thank you Judith Mara and Lynn Flannery for the ongoing partnership and unflinching marketing and web support.

Every day I get to work with amazing clients. While my job is to help them, I am constantly inspired by how they embrace opportunities and rise to the occasion and initiate positive change. The book would not be if not for you. Thank you for allowing me to work by your side as you navigate your career and life challenges.

Finally, I wouldn't be who I am today without the support of my mom and sister. Your unwavering love and strength of character guides me through all that I do.

INTRODUCTION

After having battled my way through my forties, I have become acutely aware of how challenging midlife can be. In the beginning, I thought it was just me having these struggles. That hypothesis was quickly refuted when I became immersed in my career as an executive coach. Over the past five years I have worked with hundreds of clients. Most of them are between the ages of thirty-five and fifty-five and work in corporate America. While each client is unique, with concerns and situations specific to him or her, I have begun to see commonalities and patterns. In particular, people are feeling hemmed into a life that is shrinking around them, so much so that they can't envision anything else. Their life and their prospects appear dim. I believe our forties are a pivotal juncture for how we will move forward into the next chapter of our lives. It is so crucial that ignoring it may detour us from the life we want.

I have the privilege of working with clients who are incredibly bright, talented, and thoughtful. The journeys with some have been short and others more extensive. With each new client there is a promise of helping him or her amplify his or her life and career. This is a true partnership from the get-go. I guide my clients as far as they want to go. Each client must have readiness to do the hard work and to make changes. Without the desire and drive to make change, the potential impact will be negligible. But those who are ready to take action and thoughtfully design the life they want will experience a new way of being that feels true and honest.

Amplify: To make larger, greater, or stronger. To expand in stating or describing, as by details or illustrations.

My clients have come to me through corporate assignments as well as on their own. At the core, for most, is managing their career. Their career has taken some perilous turns, and how they navigate them can result in ongoing success or failure to proceed, or even a downward spiral. When they are in it, they may get swallowed up in all the mayhem and not see the realities and possibilities. Without a vision, we can hold on for dear life and miss other opportunities. Our ability to visualize the life we want becomes further clouded with all the responsibilities (familial and financial) we accumulate along the way.

In addition to my clients, I've had the opportunity to observe and speak with a number of people about what they are experiencing and how it is impacting their life. The general consensus is that navigating midlife is much more challenging than they expected. While they think this should be when they "have it all," they quickly realize it is when they instead have to figure it out. Nothing is as they imagined. The "good life" is elusive and it's harder to attain than they thought. That is the truth, and nothing has been more disconcerting than the devastating years that rocked the world during the late 2000s. Most were impacted by these tough times, and the squeeze was particularly painful for those who found themselves sidelined in their career. Furthermore, responsibility for family is greater than ever before. According to the Pew Research Center just over one of every eight Americans aged forty to sixty is financially supporting a child over eighteen *and* caring for a parent; in addition, between seven million and ten million adults are caring for their aging parents from a long distance.[1]

Well before I entertained the idea of becoming an executive coach, I was given a piece of advice that resulted in a major shift in how I would shape my life. Shortly after I moved back to Chicago, after spending seven years in New York City, I attended a holiday party hosted by a dear friend and colleague. Also in attendance was a senior-level creative director I used to work with many years before. After a few minutes of exchanging pleasantries he said, "I want to apologize in advance if I was ever an ass to you when we worked together." Even though he had said reputation, it was never on display when we worked together. I was still a junior-level account person and although our working relationship was short-lived, it was very amiable. However, I did appreciate the sentiment. It was the next half hour that really had an impact.

He proceeded to talk about the importance of taking control of your career and being your own advocate, especially as you become more tenured. The higher you rise within an organization and the more you make, the more vulnerable you are likely to become. He found this out the hard way. Unfortunately, he was unceremoniously let go as part of a downsizing effort. This caught him completely off guard. He had ascended to a senior-level position on the merits of his prowess in building a strong, creative reputation. He was dedicated to his company and had uprooted his family a number of times in order to answer the call of his employer. Like many others, he worked long days, nights, and weekends for the benefit of his company and his client. Now, he was left scrambling to figure out what to do next. When these decisions are forced on you, they can shake your confidence and set you back professionally and emotionally. He, like others, naively believed that this would never happen to him.

There was no indication that he had lost favor within the ranks of senior leadership. His relationships with the client were strong, and he was feeling confident in his abilities. What he wasn't aware of were the political maneuverings that were taking place behind closed doors. Changes to the management team were combined with tough economic times and the need to reduce costs, in particular at the senior level. Loyalties that were once strong and abiding became tenuous or nonexistent and soon he was shown the door. He, like just about everyone in this or similar situations, was left struggling to regain his footing.

So what was his advice? Make sure *you* have control of your career and don't leave it to the whim of others. Over time, he steadied himself and found new opportunities for growth and fulfillment, but this very casual cocktail-party conversation stuck with me. At the time, I was happily ensconced in my career; however, it made me keenly aware that you have to be actively navigating your career at all times.

> *Immense power is acquired by assuring yourself in your*
> *secret reveries that you were born to control affairs.*
> —ANDREW CARNEGIE

As I worked with more and more "midlife" people, I realized there is a lack of resources for them to draw on. It seems to be a neglected decade in our lives. And yet, it is the time when people feel most vulnerable about who they are, what they want to do, and the impact they want to have. People become cognizant that the time to invoke change is now, and yet they aren't exactly sure what to do next, let alone how to do it. With my clients, I can see the distress in their faces and voices as they wrestle with issues like "What am I doing with my life?" It's a big question with no easy answer. That's why so many people push it back to the farthest recesses of their consciousness. And yet it will continue to gnaw at them, little by little, until something happens—such as losing a job, which forces them to reevaluate their current situation. Unfortunately, by then they are panicked and hastily making decisions. These usually end up being short-term fixes that do not set them up for long-term success. Frequently I hear, "I just have to find a job and will deal with those other important questions later." But when is later? When they find themselves in a miserable job? At that point, they are stuck, at least for a while, and quite often they end up feeling more disempowered and frustrated because they know they made a bad decision.

We all have had times when we were hard-pressed and made short-term career decisions (even when we knew they were misguided) in order to pay the bills and keep the home running smoothly. What this book offers is a more desirable approach that requires foresight and the ability to take initiative to gain clarity about what direction one's life is headed in. But to implement this approach, you must be proactive. I saw this frequently in business: Those who have a vision and can get out ahead of a business situation are the ones most likely to have ongoing success. The same holds true in how we manage our lives. Taking the initiative to craft a plan for your life that will guide, inform, and answer the question "What do I want to do with my life?" will set you up for a rewarding and fulfilling life.

Over the course of this book, I will lead you through the four key steps you need to take to amplify your life:

1. Interrogate where you are in your life today.

2. Formulate a plan and belief system to guide you forward.

3. Conquer the fears and saboteurs that are holding you back.

4. Adopt a way of being that supports the life you want.

When you get to the other side, you will be ready to live in a way that supports the life you want.

My goal with this book is to help those struggling to figure out these midlife years to thrive in the decades ahead. The insights and stories included here come from real clients and their situations; however, the details have been modified in order to protect confidentiality. I hope you enjoy the book and find value in the insights and tools presented. To aid in your journey, the *Amplify Your Career and Life* workbook is available on my website, www.petercdiamond.com.

KEY QUESTION

· Are you ready to amplify your career and life?

STEP ONE

INTERROGATING YOUR LIFE

CHAPTER ONE

FACING THE HARD TRUTH

We all have pivotal moments in our lives when we are dealt one devastating crisis after another. When these traumatic events come in rapid-fire succession, they can leave us dispirited at best, downtrodden at worst. Life can seem bleak when we are confronting substantial hardship, whether it is in our career, personal life, or both. When such misfortunes occur later in life, they can take on a deeper meaning and the burdens feel heavier. We find ourselves at a crossroads, and the path we take will set the stage for how the next phase of our life unfolds.

My Story

There I was, at the peak of my career. I was forty-five years old, a senior vice president at a globally renowned advertising agency, and I was in the throes of the worst year of my life. Up to that moment, I had done all the right things to get where I thought I wanted to be. I immersed myself in my career. I spent years studying the advertising business and how to succeed in it. I developed strong client and agency relationships. I did everything I could to meet the needs of others. I wanted to be associated with successful brand campaigns, so I worked sixty-hour weeks in order to ensure flawless execution and delivery. I wanted my teams to be successful, so I spent extra time ensuring that they were sufficiently trained. I wanted to be valuable to the agency, so I took on more responsibilities in addition to running my accounts. I wanted to do everything right in order to not feel exposed.

To do everything "right," I made personal sacrifices. I did not make plans during the week just in case there was a client emergency or I had to work late. I did not plan vacations because I did not want to miss a client meeting. I would stay connected 24/7 in case someone needed something. I was putting the agency and my clients ahead of myself. I was doing it so I could make more money and have more status, the bigger office, and of course the coveted parking space. It was a bit like a drug. The more I got, the more I wanted. A bigger bump, another hit. And yet I was constantly surrounded by the risk that it could all be taken away in a matter of seconds.

I was also working in an environment with others who were just like me, so we fed off each other and competed with each other. We all had the same thought: What do I have to do to get to the next promotion? The elusive carrot was always there, and we all had to constantly jockey for a limited number of positions at the top. In most situations, we had to be our own best champion and self-promoter. Those with the biggest accounts, the loudest voice, or savviest political skills were reaping the great rewards. And we were only as good as our last big win. But this was the game we knew we had signed up for.

Advertising is a young person's business. It is grueling and all-consuming. If you do not make your move up before you are fifty, it is basically not going to happen. This was supposed to be the time when my life came together, when I could claim all my long-awaited rewards: position, money, corporate and professional power. So, I was pushing forward.

I would look around and think, "I am as smart and capable as my peers or anyone leading this or other agencies where I have worked. I am told I have all the right skills. I am told that I have no controlling weaknesses. I am told it is just a matter of time and there are just a few things to work on." So, I soldiered on to become the complete agency guy. I took on additional accounts (the unglamorous ones). I undertook more initiatives to improve our processes as well as a training program for young, talented agency folks. In the absence of any other purpose, I worked to accomplish more and to keep pushing up the corporate ladder. But for some reason, I was not moving up. Why not? Why had I stalled? What was going on?

Something was holding me back from being firmly committed to doing all that was required. There was a nagging voice in my head that was questioning whether this was really what I wanted and who I wanted to be in order to get it. While I had sacrificed my time, did I really want to sacrifice who I was in order to climb up one more rung of the corporate ladder? I began to realize that at that level it was more than just getting to the next promotion.

I began to question whether this was the right career for me moving forward. What if my professional success was about something more than just winning awards and bottom-line results? I know now that success equals the reconciliation of one's personal and professional values. That was something I hadn't considered or really cared about in the past. While I didn't even have clarity on my personal values, I knew I was disheartened and in a precarious state.

The year that followed had all the makings of a Greek tragedy. No dramatic trope was left untriggered: career upheaval, suffering, illness, and death. It started in April, when my big account decided to pull support from all the brands in my portfolio. Full stop. When the call came, I felt the blood drain from my face and my stomach tighten. Their decision was devastating. I hung up the phone in disbelief. A less-than-five-minute conversation would result in hundreds of hours of damage control. It was a business choice about the allocation of the client's resources; it had nothing to do with how we were servicing the account, the quality of our creative product, or the state of the relationship. But that did not make me feel any better. This was a character-building moment for me.

But I did not think about me; I thought about my team and their well-being. Very quickly, I pulled them together and delivered the most difficult speech of my life: *I regret to inform you that starting today the account we've been dedicated to is no longer supporting the brands we work on, but do not worry, we are going to do everything we can to find positions for everyone.* These colleagues had been close associates for many years and there was nothing more agonizing than looking out at a room filled with forty-five shell-shocked faces. When something ends so abruptly, it sends shivers down your spine. People get very concerned about their jobs. In advertising, when you lose an account, in most cases there will be job losses. As they filed out of the room, people congratulated me for how I handled the situation. I still felt as though I had let them down, even though it wasn't a reflection of my leadership.

While I was taking care of the forty-five people on my team, I realized that I too was feeling vulnerable, exposed. There were passing hallway promises that I would be kept on my current account until I found a spot for myself, but it would not be a long-term solution and I would have to find a new position. So I was forced to ask myself, what do I want to do? I needed to start interrogating my life.

At that point, I did what I always do in the midst of change—hunker

down and start working the internal agency system to see what opportunities are available. However, this time, it felt different. I was forced
to dig deep into the well of my inner being. There was some serious
soul-searching to be done. I had to ask myself, how do I want to be,
what do I want from my career, and most important, what impact do I
want to have beyond my current four walls? I had wrestled with these
questions before, but this time, there was a new sense of urgency to find
the answers. Time was pressing on me. Time had never been an affordable
luxury for me, but I had yet to realize exactly how precious it could be.

★ ★ ★

While this storm was tossing me about, my personal life was in for a
major shake-up as well. I have always been adept at keeping work and my
personal life separate. In fact, I had ruthlessly marginalized my personal
life in order to accommodate work. This year, my personal and professional lives were on a collision course.

Earlier in the year, my mom had been having serious health issues.
After a number of surgeries over the course of the year, this once-active
eighty-one-year-old would eventually take residence in an assisted living
home. Even more heartrending, my forty-eight-year-old brother died of
a massive heart attack over Memorial Day weekend. In less than twelve
hours we had lost a great husband, father, brother, son, and gregarious
soul. It was so unexpected and surreal.

On May 21, around 10 p.m., I received a call from my panic-stricken
sister-in-law. It was unusual for her to call me directly, and almost as soon
as I answered, she started asking me rapid-fire questions about my dad
and his death some thirty-one years earlier. I was confused and trying
to make sense of this line of questioning and what was happening. My

sister-in-law explained that less than an hour earlier, my brother had had a seizure while watching TV. He was rushed to a nearby hospital to be treated for cardiac arrest. At the same time, the medical staff was trying to gain as much medical background and family history as they could in order to help save his life.

I rattled off as much as I could remember about the cause of my father's death. As I spoke, I felt this strange wedge forcing itself between reality and disbelief. I tried to lock my brain into the situation in order to be helpful, but I couldn't keep from getting sidetracked with thoughts that this wasn't really happening. I had just spoken to my brother two days prior. He sounded a bit stressed but nothing concerning. The phone call with my brother's wife lasted long enough for me to provide the needed information, and then she was gone. I was left standing alone 250 miles away in a state of shock, trying to make sense of what was happening. To complicate matters, I had been out drinking after work and was in no shape to get in a car and drive. I had to wait until the next morning to be with my family. My sister, who lived near my brother, went to the hospital and kept me posted with developments throughout the night.

My brother's condition had not improved by morning, so at the crack of dawn, I got in my car and headed east. About forty-five minutes into my journey, my sister called with an update. I immediately knew the news was not good. Her voice betrayed her.

"I think you should pull over," she said.

"No, just tell me."

"I think you should pull over," she said again.

But I couldn't. I had to keep going. Keep moving, I thought. My eyes were blurring from the tears, but my adrenaline was racing. My brother dying was not an option. My father survived his first heart attack at the same age as my brother and he would do the same. Built with a strong body and a never-say-never attitude, he was bound to come through. But I was wrong.

I still had three and a half hours of driving time to process what had happened. With the highway virtually free of other cars and the cloudless sky an incredible shade of blue, I drove on while my mind went somewhere else. Although I was moving forward, I felt suspended in time. Everything felt out of place. Intellectually, I couldn't comprehend what had happened or its transformative effect.

Just past the halfway point in the drive, I finally came to grips with what the next three or four days would look like. There was one conversation that needed to take place that would test my resolve . . .

And that's when two two-by-fours came flying directly at the windshield of my car. With my reflexes already working in auxiliary power, coupled with the speed at which the boards were traveling through the air, I was unable to maneuver the car out of the way. The first one bounced off the front grill of my car, and the second hit the driver side of the windshield before bouncing off the roof. "What the f**k!!!" I exclaimed to my passengerless car. Really, what kind of message was being sent? Given the rate at which the two-by-fours were flying and the speed of my car, there probably is a better than 50 percent chance at least one of them would have busted through the windshield. Where had they come from and how had I survived?

I needed to regroup. I got off at the next exit to inspect the damage to my car. Not surprisingly, the front grill was pretty beat up and there was damage to the roof. Shockingly, there wasn't even a crack in the windshield. A sign? Maybe. But how many signs does one need? I composed myself and made my way back onto the highway. For the next ninety minutes I reflected on my brother's death and what could have been a life-ending injury for me.

But nothing would prepare me for the most gut-wrenching of all conversations: having to tell my mother that her son had died.

I met my sister at her house before we were to speak with my mother. We embraced and comforted each other, knowing that our collective strength was needed in order to keep it together, especially for my mother. At the time, my mother was in a rehab center recovering from knee replacement surgery. While the surgeon deemed it a success, my mother struggled with the protracted recovery, leaving her dispirited. We arrived at the rehab center, and I steeled myself to face my mother. While everything around me was happening at its usual pace, I felt as though I was moving in slow motion. The hallway seemed to extend forever and voices were muffled. All I kept thinking was that everyone else was having a normal Friday. Not us. Nothing would be normal for a long time.

My sister and I hadn't discussed who would say what, but it naturally happened that I (the youngest sibling) would deliver the news. Upon my entrance into her room, my mother was surprised to see me and greeted me with a warm smile and a hello. "I didn't know you were coming into town." I couldn't respond. Instead, I continued to approach her, kiss her cheek, and kneel at the side of her wheelchair. "Mom, there's something I have to tell you . . . " my voice quivered. And there it was. The look of disbelief and the veil of blackness that came over her will be forever embedded in my memory. They say there is nothing more tragic than for a parent to outlive her child. The same is true for having to tell your parent that one of her children has died. This will be with me forever.

As I see it, two factors contributed to my brother's death: work-related stress and poor health. These factors also led to my father's death at the age of fifty-four. After my brother passed away, the frailties of health and life were weighing on me heavily. They would influence how I would approach my life and career.

Not only was my mental state fragile but the physical stress, strain, and negligence began to take a toll on my body as well. In June, I injured my shoulder playing tennis. In true fashion, I ignored my pain and decided not to go to the doctor because I was too busy with work and family issues. For three months, I struggled through the pain, thinking it would get better on its own. I finally came to my senses and went to the doctor in September. One MRI later, and lo and behold, I had a severely torn rotator cuff. It was so bad my doctors immediately scheduled the surgery before there was any further damage. Apparently, I have a high tolerance for pain.

Did I have to be assaulted so many times over such a short period for me to turn what had been in my heart into action? Unfortunately, I think the answer is yes. To get through to me across the clamor of corporate politics, aging parents, frailty of life, and living in an aging body, the universe was sending a loud and clear message to me.

I took notice.

★ ★ ★

My first step in changing my life was to take a closer look at my career. Until then, I viewed my career as a bit of a struggle. The more time I spent in advertising, the less grounded I felt. I could see the potential career options within my current company and industry, but none of them were really creating a spark of energy. None of them were exciting to me. None of them were something I was looking forward to. In fact, the prospects were weighing me down. I stubbornly held on to the notion that I should be doing something more with my career and life. I was not ready to accept that this stasis was it. I was not ready to decelerate through the next stage of my career and just wait it out, thinking that I would figure it out later. I wanted a vision—a vision that was open with possibilities and did not end with the next promotion.

Discovering what that vision was became my quest. When I started this journey to reclaim who I was, I made a pact with myself that I would put it all out there, even the ugly stuff I kept out of reach from others. I also submitted to the help of others: a coach, friends, colleagues, a therapist, and family. I knew that left to my own devices, I would not do the hard labor required but rather push it off to the side for later. Thankfully, this time I trusted myself to pursue my personal mission—to help others, specifically those who are dealing with similar life issues.

This personal mission led me to a new career as an executive coach. The shift came as a result of my exploring what I wanted and how I wanted to live my life. I started by drawing a connective line among my strengths, my career successes, and my interests. I determined that I want to have a positive impact on people and create hope in their lives. To do this, I had to let go of all the things I was doing that I thought were the "right" things to do. That included leaving the world of advertising and, to some degree, corporate America. With that exit came mourning the loss of some unfulfilled corporate goals: title, perks, prestige. Instead, I wanted to focus on how to live my life based on my personal vision, purpose, and values. I wanted to be guided by my own core belief system, a way of being that would guide me through any situation. A personal creed that would propel me toward what I want rather than living a life in which I was always moving away from what I did not want.

This was an interesting and profound shift for me. In the past, I would try something and discard it if it didn't suit me. I was constantly moving away from the "bad." I had not yet articulated what was "good"—what I really wanted and how I wanted to live my life. I never had a true vision of my future; it was always gray, mushy, and nebulous.

My story is not unique. Many of us begin to see a downward slide sometime during our forties. The rigors of life, family, and career begin to take hold and really wear us down. We see our light begin to fade and our energy wane. We find ourselves giving in to others and not stepping forward for what we believe. It is just too much to navigate. It is exhausting. Because of our obligations, it is easier to downshift and go along in order to maintain and retain what we have.

I, like you, wanted to break my cycle, make a change, and amplify my life. I wanted to live an informed life based on my vision for the future. Once I cleared away all the distractions, I was better able to focus and move forward with confidence and conviction.

KEY QUESTIONS I ASKED MYSELF AT THE END OF THIS YEAR

- What have I been doing because I thought it was the "right" thing to do?
- How am I going to respond to the events that happened this year?
- What would my life be like if I was moving toward what I want versus away from what I don't?

No matter your career, no matter your age, no matter what you have or have not achieved thus far in your life, there is no time like the present to dig deep and reclaim your life. I am not saying it will be easy. And I am definitely not saying it will happen overnight. But what I am saying is you owe it to yourself to reclaim who you are and what you want. It will not only pay dividends to you, but it will also positively impact those around you. Are you ready?

CHAPTER TWO

WHAT IS THE ARC OF YOUR LIFE?

Now that you have heard a bit of my story and the year that changed my life, it's time to find out what is happening in your life. The answer will be the basis for how you move forward.

What is motivating you to take a closer look at the way you have been living? Are you driven by a specific event or events, or have you simply realized that you no longer feel connected to who you are and what you want? Perhaps there is an overwhelming desire to confront what is happening in your life. The emotional intensity you're feeling is too great to will away. Or perhaps there is another force you have to reckon with: time. As you get a little older, you realize that time and the years of unrestrained health are becoming precious. This is when you begin to internalize that a shift is taking place and action is required.

But first, how did you get here?

Working as a coach, I see common patterns of behavior that emerge in our lives. They form an arc that begins to take shape in adulthood. While that arc is as unique as our own DNA, there are shared experiences among us. Let's first take a visual look at a typical life arc. As you can see in the graph that follows, there is an upward trajectory beginning in one's twenties that continues through one's thirties, but it begins to level off or even decline as one experiences one's forties. Certain pivotal events during these decades shape the arc of our lives.

ARC OF YOUR LIFE

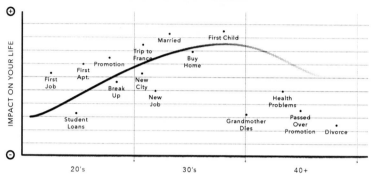

Life as a Free Agent: Our Twenties

For most of us, life's true journey begins in our early twenties. It is the decade of firsts. The focus is on the physicality of life and the very act of putting ourselves out there and doing. During this time, we are freeing ourselves from the confines of family and school and beginning to assert ourselves as independent, decision-making adults. With that, we set out to explore and to live life. We feel free. There is not much downside to our decisions; if we do not like what we're doing, or where we are, we can reboot.

Our environment plays a vital role in shaping the beginning of this arc: where we live, the job we have, and the friends we have picked up along the way. There is a tidal wave of excitement that sweeps us up. Every day is a new exploration and we have the stamina to conquer it. There is not much permanence to our lives. The thought of giving meaning to what we are doing is probably surface level at best. We get our first job. If we do not like it, that is okay; we get a new one. Or we go back to school. Or we take the summer off. If we like our job and the company wants to transfer us to a different city, or we take an overseas assignment or a special project with insane hours, cool. We are going with the flow and we are staking our career and life on limited knowledge of the "outside" world and ourselves.

More than likely, we have stumbled into a career. It may be a career that we thought would provide a good living, or was respectable, or that our family strongly urged us to consider. This makes sense. How else would we know what to try? Some people figure out early on exactly what they are meant to do, but they are in the minority (and probably not reading this book). When I left undergrad I was driven by the need to have a practical degree in order to ensure I got a job, made money, and paid my student loans. At the time, in the early eighties, some of the popular careers were engineering, accounting, law, and medicine. They were all deemed practical or "right," since you acquired specific technical skills and put them to use for above-average pay. Very few of my peers, at the time, chose a liberal arts degree. None of those jobs paid more than $12,000 yearly. While I was not thrilled with any of the "right" options, I was very concerned with being practical and getting a decent-paying job. While my father worked a blue-collar professional job as a supervisor of electrical illustration at Ford Motor Company in Detroit, most of my aunts and uncles were self-employed, and I had no clue what it would be like in the corporate working world.

I chose accounting because it was practical, there were plenty of jobs, and I had an aptitude for it. And I stress the word *aptitude*. Not passion, keen interest, or even mild enthusiasm. I attended Michigan State University, which had one of the top accounting departments, and I knew I

23

would be able to land a job after college. So there I was, slogging through and being very practical, because it was the "right" thing to do. Thankfully, halfway through my junior year, I realized I had no desire to be a CPA, so I took myself off that track and focused on corporate accounting and finance. At that point, all that mattered was graduating and getting a job.

A curious thing happened two weeks after I started my first corporate job. The company I worked for, a big computer mainframe manufacturer, had a massive layoff of two thousand people. From my office window, I saw people who I hadn't met yet, along with former coworkers, streaming into the streets, carrying cardboard boxes full of their personal belongings—plants were sticking out of the tops of the boxes, and each face was wearing a shell-shocked expression. Dotted in the background were EMS vehicles waiting in the wings. From what I could tell, there was no warning, and genuine dismay pervaded the hallways of the corporate headquarters. The new realities of corporate America—here today, gone tomorrow—were becoming apparent. The impact on me at the time was minimal. I still had my job. But it did leave an uneasy feeling that has forever made me cautious about what to expect from an employer.

But it's not all about career in our twenties. We experience many other life events and transformations as well: travel, more serious romantic relationships, marriage, children, job loss, car purchase, apartments and new homes. It is the decade of firsts. We are rolling through it without really checking in with ourselves.

I Want More: Our Thirties

The arc of our life continues upward. In our thirties, we set out to conquer. Anything is possible. There is arrogance about what we will do and what we are capable of. Life is full steam ahead, and we are amassing obligations left, right, and center. Our ambitions are high and we strive for success. We have also begun to establish our roots and routine. We feel strong, like we're really getting somewhere. We have moved from the decade of firsts to the decade of "I want more."

Our days are now filled by professional and personal obligations. We have declared our plan, and we are going to do everything we can to execute it. We have made some key decisions about our career, our relationships, and how we see our lives playing out. And typically, the execution of the plan depends on the "right" way to do it—how we are expected to do it. So if we get married, we have kids. If we have kids, we buy a house. If we buy a house, it is in the suburbs. If we don't have kids, we take a place in a trendy neighborhood with all the upgrades. If we have settled on a career and company, we follow the path. How we execute our lives is mostly influenced by our external environment. And it is happening almost by rote. Life is transpiring fast, and there is not much time to question it due to all the demands of career and family.

By this point, most of us have risen above the junior ranks and are smack in the middle management of an organization. This means we have been given real responsibility and probably have a voice that is being heard. We may even be identified and groomed for true leadership roles within the organization. For me, this was when I ran the day-to-day operations of an account at a large advertising agency. My boss was pretty hands-off and she let me run with it. I represented the agency in most of our client meetings and worked closely with the creative director. We basically made the decisions and were responsible for the account. And I loved that responsibility and ownership. If you are like me, you want more.

By now, it has been instilled in us that to maintain this life, we have to do it all and be pretty near perfect. So, what does perfection look like? You are probably working forty to fifty-five hours a week. You probably spend at least two hours commuting to and from work. You probably have to be tethered to your job even when you are at home, answering emails and texts, or taking phone calls. You probably have a house to manage. You probably have a spouse who needs some attention (although I am guessing this is relegated to somewhere near the bottom of the list). You probably have kids who have homework, sports, music, and other activities that require your attention. You probably have family obligations, weddings, baptisms, bar mitzvahs, birthday parties, and holiday gatherings. You probably have at least one other family member who requires your attention. You probably have at least one health issue that has surfaced that you may or may not be treating. You probably want to spend time with your friends for golf, book club, poker, or having lunch. This is also probably relegated to the bottom of your list. You probably belong to a church or volunteer. And who knows, you may even want a little time to yourself to go for a run, read, or relax in peace and quiet—which is probably dead last on your list. When you put all this together, perfection looks more like doing for others and less like doing for yourself.

Our thirties have become an unstoppable whir of activity. And because most of what is happening is positive, there isn't much cause for reflection or concern. We are gaining and adding to our lives. We are building our confidence, and even arrogance, as an adult. We are establishing our own traditions and beliefs. We have settled down and taken root. Everything is growing: our salary, our family, our belongings, our experiences, our maturity, and our capacity to take on and manage more responsibilities.

For most of us during this decade, an enormous number of activities pull us in many directions. But we aren't aware of what's beginning to chip away at us. We are not in a position to notice that creating *more* is not necessarily better. With every new responsibility we assume, something else in our lives has to be sacrificed.

Fraying at the Edges: Our Forties

When we reach our forties, it is as if everything begins to slow down and the looming crisis point floats closer. Here, we realize that we have collected a lot of data about our lives. We have probably had a couple of career moves and a variety of jobs. We are in, or have been in, romantic relationships. If we have kids, they have probably reached a point where they either are, or are getting to be, self-sufficient. And our family relationships have undoubtedly had some twists and turns. As we slow down, we begin to take stock and ask ourselves certain tough questions, like "What am I doing?" "Who am I?" and "Where am I going?" These are three very scary questions. It may be that these kinds of questions have circled our thoughts before, but until recently we have had so much going on that it was easy to compartmentalize and ignore them—they begin to nag at us. Now, we feel our life is beginning to fray.

For most, this is when true hardships emerge: loss of job, loss of family, loss of health, loss of wealth, loss of focus, loss of belief, loss of purpose (which we probably never truly had). We are realizing more losses than gains. And often, our careers are sitting at the front and center of our focus. It is where we spend the most physical and emotional energy. It is the financial life line that pushes us forward.

In such circumstances, many of us feel less fulfilled than ever. Our

27

lives have slowed down a bit and we are looking around and wondering, *Is this really where I fit in?* This is also a time of great internal struggle. I have learned that most people believe that doing what they want to do and having financial success can't work in concert with each other. Truth be told, I shared this belief. The center of this dilemma is that most people have never clearly articulated what they want.

Exercise: Your Life Arc

Mapping your own life arc can help you see where you have been and where you are heading. When you know that, you will be in a position to make a change. Plot the arc of your life on a piece of paper. What are your key milestones in your twenties, thirties, and forties? What was the impact of each milestone on your life? Was it positive or negative? How was your arc trending ten years ago? How is your arc trending today? Why?

Career in Flux: Is This It?

"My life is slowing down and my career is not turning out as I had hoped. Now what do I want to do?" This big, open-ended question leaves most people paralyzed. It is daunting. We are not accustomed to actively controlling our careers and seeking work that will inspire and enrich us. We don't know where to begin, so we leave it up to chance. Throughout my years of coaching, I have seen three converging paths. On one road are those who think their employer will have their best interests in mind and take care of them. "If I do a good job, they will always have a job for me. If I do a good job, I will be rewarded. If I do a good job, I will be challenged." These people are waiting for others to lead the way.

On the second are those who jump around from job to job hoping to find the elusive perfect job. "If I do not like how I am being treated, I will leave. If I think I should be paid more, I will leave. If I am not learning, I will leave." These people are moving away from what they do not like.

On the third road are those who had been living the life they wanted but now, faced with shifting priorities, have to reevaluate where they will go from here. Their position is being eliminated or moved to another office. They are no longer a two-income household. A family member needs financial and emotional support. These people are at a standstill while they reassess their current situation.

Perhaps the most difficult part about finding our career in flux is that this is the time when we have the most to give. We have a wealth of twenty-plus years of experience to draw upon. We have cultivated a certain level of expertise and knowledge, and we can effectively lead and manage because we can anticipate the rough patches. We know how to maneuver through the political landscape of an organization, big or small. And yet, many of us are feeling pinched. The young, up-and-coming folks have more technical skills, exuberant energy, and lower salaries. But more important, we no longer see how we fit into the organization. We grapple with knowing if the organization considers us high-potential employees who will continue to be rewarded and given challenging assignments. And whether this is consistent with how we rate our contributions and value to the company.

Some organizations make it clear whether or not an employee is viewed as senior-level material, and I am talking the top 10 to 15 percent. These are the truly coveted positions that garner the most financial wealth and prestige. If you're being groomed for one of these positions you know it, and if you aren't, well, you know that too. At other companies it is never quite clear who's in and who's out. Workers are never told where their future lies, so they often cling to the notion "no news is good news." The train of thought goes like this: "They must like me because they have not told me they do not. I may not be progressing like my peers, but my performance reviews are usually pretty good. The few recurring themes that have come up I have easily explained, ignored, or dismissed." Life is fine when you live with your head down.

For me, while I always had very strong evaluations, I had two recurring themes: not being a risk taker and not being tough enough. Although there is some truth to both of these, it was more circumstantial than germane to who I am. I believe in fair negotiations, and my personal leadership style is to treat people with respect, which to some is a sign of weakness. When these issues came up yet again during my very last performance evaluation in 2009, I finally put it on the table and said, "This is who I am and this is my leadership style. If the agency requires something different, maybe it is time for us to part ways." Not surprising, there was plenty of backpedaling and nothing much more came of it. However, I realized that this was one more aspect of my life that was beginning to fray. That conversation was one of many that convinced me I needed to take my career and future success into my own hands and out of the hands of my bosses or the agency.

Years later, I am taking risks, starting a new career, starting my own business, writing this book. Maybe I just was not passionate enough about what I was doing to warrant the risks. Discovering this fact was a breakthrough—an "aha" moment for me. I can and do take risks, I just have to believe in them. That is how our core belief system works—that system of vision, values, and purpose that guides us.

There is no perfect job and there is no one who truly has your best interest in mind except yourself. I believe there is a lot of intellectual capital that is not being fully utilized among the forty- to fifty-year-olds. Because of this, these workers are feeling marginalized, jaded by the system, or frustrated with what to do next.

This should be the time when we are standing in our full power in terms of both career and family. For many, however, it is when we really begin to question ourselves: "What am I doing with my career and—gasp—my life?" This crisis may be of our own doing, or it may be that the rug was just pulled out from under us via layoffs, poor health, divorce, or simple career stagnation. Either way, there is little doubt that our forties look different from our twenties and thirties. We need to embrace the truth that we are older and wiser. We need to leverage our experiences and what we know about ourselves to set us up for the next ten to twenty years. And while this time may feel like the beginning of the end, I say it's the start of a new beginning.

KEY QUESTIONS

- Have you been proactive or reactive in living your life?
- Have you been doing what's "right" or what's right for you?
- How have recent events affected your life arc?
- Are you ready for a new beginning?

CHAPTER THREE

ARE YOU FEELING BOXED IN?

As I coached more people within the context of their current career, I was shocked to find out how many people in the latter stages of their careers are just gutting it out and waiting for the time when they can do what they really want to do. I define "latter stages" as having fifteen to twenty years' experience: for most, it is the midpoint of their career. By this time you have significant knowledge and insight about yourself, your career, and your ambitions. The question is what do you do with it and when.

Many people let their accumulated knowledge and insight go unnoticed, especially when touting it would entail change. They push aside and confine their awareness to a narrow reality that is directly in front of them. The horizon is measured in mere feet and their peripheral view is almost nonexistent. In essence, they are closing down a longer-term view of opportunities and growth by building a protective fortress around what they know now. It's a superbly used defense mechanism that maintains the status quo. But if there is one thing we know, it's that change is happening around us even if we choose not to participate. When people confine themselves to a false reality that is distorting their line of sight, they may end up in a world of hurt both financially and emotionally. Unfortunately, it's far easier to build a protective fortress than it is to honestly interrogate where you are today and use that as a launching point for formulating an action plan to move forward. We have saboteurs to conquer (more about these in chapter 7) and ways of being to adopt before we can achieve this great change, but we have to start somewhere.

The key to integrating accumulated knowledge and insights into action is awareness. Knowledge and insight will serve no purpose if you are not aware of them. To create awareness, you have to have the ability and presence of mind to step back and see your current situation for what it is. This includes your career, your life, and your health. In an ideal state, by having awareness, you would be able to paint a clear picture of your current situation. In reality, you probably are not ready for the complete truth. You are ready, however, to find the threads of truth. By relying on intuition or gut instincts, you generally know when something is not going well. Not only do you know it in your mind, but you also know it in your body. Do you have a uncomfortable pit in your stomach? Are your shoulders hunched over? Are your palms sweaty every time you are around certain people or asked to do certain tasks? Does your heart start to beat a little faster in these situations? These are all physical signs of distress.

While lack of action may protect you from getting hurt or being vulnerable, it also has a huge impact on your health and relationships. If you push aside what you know is true about your current job situation, you usually end up compensating for it in other ways. This could be eating too much in order to make you feel good or not enough as a means of maintaining control over something. You may indulge in vices such as liquor or drugs as a way of taking the edge off. You may overwork yourself by staying late at the office, signaling how dedicated you are but also keeping you away from your family. You may become so single-focused around work that you have no other interests. The impact of these actions can wreak havoc on your body and your family while stoking the fire of resentment that is burning inside.

Bringing awareness to a situation and the truths that exist will help you take action. Awareness may be nothing more than a realization that your current situation is no longer serving you and something has to change. Actually, this is a huge step forward. Now you can really begin to put your knowledge and insight to good use. Unfortunately, this is also when you might start treading water because you do not know what to do next.

Understanding where you are is essential in being able to shape an action plan to move forward, and an accurate and thorough self-assessment will help you gain that understanding. When your arc begins to turn downward you may panic and look for quick-fix solutions, such as blaming others (your job or company) and hastily seeking employment elsewhere. This will only mask the problem without addressing the heart of the issue. Instead, you must uncover and bring awareness to the core issue so that you can take accountability and make progress.

Many people, when asked, are unable to articulate what they really want to do with their lives. They sidestep the question. Or they answer it in terms of their current job. Indeed, it can be a difficult question to answer. Most people have not given it much thought because they are riding the merry-go-round and they cannot slow down long enough to think. When they dig deeper, another, more fundamental issue presents the biggest obstacle: The answer may result in their having to take action outside their comfort zone. Often people hide behind the excuse "I have financial responsibilities and I need to get through the next ten years," or "however long it takes to get the kids through college and save enough for retirement." What people are not realizing is that while they are pushing through the next ten or so years, they are actively relinquishing control over who they are and what they want. They have decided to settle and focus on trying to survive. What they sacrifice is the greater opportunity to thrive. If they are gutting it out and confined in a fortress, they are probably not enjoying their career.

This is troubling to me. As I see it, it is a terrible waste of human capital. A vast wealth of skills and experience are being underutilized. But why? Have people simply given in to the corporate system? One factor to consider is the inner workings of corporate America, in which the smartest or best leaders are not always those who rise to the top. In truth and in practice, it is those who are smart but also adept at navigating the political terrain who gain the most recognition. The old adage "It is not what you know but who you know" reigns supreme. This is a struggle for the humble leaders who believe their work should speak for itself, or who don't want to succumb to using puffery in order to advance their career. They constantly find themselves sitting outside the upper echelons of many organizations.

Corporations are highly competitive, and those people with the best political skills usually push ahead. They tend to be the ones who build critical relationships and are gifted at saying the "right" things. The "right" things may not be reality, but they sound awfully darn good, especially if they promise a bright future. When times are prosperous, there is plenty to go around and politics become muted. There is more camaraderie and congeniality. Everybody gets to share in the wealth and the friendship. But when times are tough and the pressure is turned up, the gloves come off—and a lot of people find themselves looking for a new job.

The culture of a company also plays a significant role in how people can manage their careers and gain success. Some cultures push people into survival mode by providing a very thin support network, especially during tough times. Alliances become key, and the battle of attrition can be intense. Those who aren't savvy enough to maneuver the cultural norms may be left in a lonely place.

Everyone has knowledge and insight about the culture of the company they work for and how it impacts them. This is a great time to bring awareness to how your company's culture is affecting you at work and at home. Do you feel as though you are swimming upstream, or are you in lockstep with your team and how it operates? Do you feel good about your position and your contributions? Do you enjoy going to work each morning? Do you feel energized at the end of the day? These are the types of questions you need to be honestly asking yourself, so that you can have the life you want. I am thankful that for most of my career in advertising I really liked what I was doing. I liked the people. I liked the product. I liked how it made me a well-rounded person. I liked the opportunities it provided. Most days, I relished going to work. And most days, I left exhausted but with a feeling of accomplishment. While I loved what I was doing and would not have done it differently, I was collecting knowledge and insight that supported my suspicion that my days as an advertising executive were coming to an end. If I am truthful, the awareness was there for a number of years. I just kept putting off the hard questions until I was pushed to the brink. If I have one regret it is that I did not have someone pushing and prodding me to honestly answer two basic questions: What do I want to do? How can it benefit a company? Now it is your turn. Are you ready to interrogate your life?

The Seven W.A.R.N.I.N.G. Signs of Distress

So here you are. Recent events, whether personal or economic, have left you unsettled and your gut is confirming that your life arc is on a downward slope. It is much earlier than you planned, but you are being forced to take a hard look at where you are in your life. While everyone's situation is highly personal, some common themes are consistent with what many people experience. I refer to them as the Seven W.A.R.N.I.N.G. Signs of Distress. You may recognize one or more of them from your own career. They are:

· **W**avering Self-Confidence
· **A**t Sea
· **R**elinquished Identity
· **N**eglected
· **I**dling
· **N**o Focus
· **G**rowing Discontent

Simon, Ethan, Miguel, Marina, Danielle, Anna, and Patrick each experienced these seven states of being before determining to make a change. We will meet these folks again later in the book. Let us start by getting a snapshot of what was happening to their arc.

Wavering Self-Confidence

With this warning sign, you question what you are doing and why. You have put pressure on yourself to succeed as defined by others, but you have never felt completely satisfied in your career choice, instead questioning the benefit you provide. After years of doing something you don't love, often for companies that held unrealistic expectations, you have a diluted sense of worth. In turn, you are uncertain about your value and cautious about finding the career you want.

Simon had been forced to start his job search. He worked in an industry that was decimated by technology and low-cost providers. There was a massive consolidation, but his twenty-plus years of impeccable work allowed him to withstand the hemorrhaging of talent that surrounded him. Eventually he, too, was forced to turn off the lights. His career path had taken him to a position of management, but one that he struggled to fully embrace. Upon the demise of his last employer, he decided it was time to pursue a career within a field he loved. This meant going back to school and inevitably taking a lower salary.

Simon had always been an excellent student both in school and in his profession. He learned his craft and was well regarded within his field. Even with all this success, he was unable to shake his apprehensions. While these apprehensions were masked in his last profession by his technical abilities and the personal relationships he formed, they were exposed as he shifted his career. In his heart he knew what he wanted to do; however, he was constantly stricken by thoughts of what he "should" be doing and the prospect of failing at this juncture in his life.

His family were ardent supporters of his choices but also concerned that his intended career might be hard to break into for someone in his forties. It was a business where you start young with low pay and work your way up. This can be daunting when you are accustomed to living a certain life.

Simon needed to reconcile his fears with his dreams. For someone who had struggled with his place and professional choices, this was leading to a lot of anxiety.

Are you struggling to recover your self-confidence in order to pursue the career you want?

At Sea

This warning sign arises when you realize you have stopped advancing and growing in your career. You are no longer learning and feeling challenged. In many cases, your career has lulled you into complacency. You have been a good soldier, performing as expected and thus, allowing others to control your destiny. In doing so, you have not actively managed your career. Your motto has been *Go along to get along*. But when something forces you to finally look around, you discover your job has become something you never wanted it to be. Worse, you have been abandoned to figure things out on your own.

Ethan, like many other folks, stumbled into his career. A degree in philosophy and an interest in people's behavior initially led him to marketing. Not really knowing what marketing was all about but knowing that he needed a job, Ethan enlisted his college friend to help him find an entry-level position. With that, the journey began. All was good for many years. A smart, analytical, and dedicated employee, he moved through the company ranks and eventually ran the research department. A string of promotions and favorable reviews kept his engine stoked. The company had plotted his career and he did as he was told with minimal resistance. This was all worthwhile because he enjoyed and respected the people on his team.

Ethan was a great guy. He believed in his company and his colleagues. There was no shortage of long nights, but there was also the camaraderie of drinking a few beers at the end of a long week. Over the years, he became known for his functional expertise and also his management skills. His team praised him for being a supportive boss with a vision for where the team was headed. If there was one chink in his leadership style, it was that he gave away too much of his power by taking on work that others should do. He felt the need to always be present on the off chance that he was needed. This meant that he was spending too much time being around for others and not enough time focusing on what was right for him. While this provided a safety net for the team, it wasn't helping to advance Ethan's agenda. In fact, he didn't have an agenda because he was spending too much time supporting others.

Executive changes began to occur at his company and they ushered in a wave of new people. With new people came a new way of operating and new dynamics that felt foreign to Ethan. Looking around the office, he felt as though strangers had infiltrated his work domain. The cadence and rhythm of what was had been lost. Ethan was not sure he liked the new vibe. He felt blindsided. With no one left to direct him, he could feel his career beginning to stagnate. While these changes did not happen quickly, the compounding effect was monumental. In no time, an acute desire to get out was mounting, but this was all he had known.

Are you feeling lost at sea and faced with making career decisions for the first time?

Relinquished Identity

Scratching and clawing your way to the top can result in losing sight of who you are. I see this happening a lot with people who are "first-generation" corporate leaders. You are the first in your family to go to college and land a corporate job that takes you into senior management. Your eagerness to be successful can be blinding. Without an early role model you can quickly latch on to how others in status positions behave. You begin to sacrifice yourself in order to fit in and be part of the club.

Miguel was from a solid middle-class family and the only one in his family to go to college. Throughout his career, he was rewarded for being very diligent and hardworking. His work ethic was seeded in childhood. But from the moment he stepped into corporate America, he felt as though he was going to be found out and his real identity unveiled—that of a blue-collar kid who lucked his way into a Big Ten school. To compensate, he felt the need to emulate and work longer and harder than others. The hard work was never an issue; however, the emulating others was more concerning. He was conflicted with what he believed to be proper comportment and how others in senior positions were behaving. But he assumed that they must know how to be; he would mirror them. Early on in his career, this wasn't as much of a problem. As he became more tenured, he was seeing the greater disconnect between what he believed and the beliefs of those around him. Lingering in the recesses of his mind, however, was a low-grade questioning of his background and professional acumen. This was a guy from the wrong side of town without the pedigree. These other folks must know what they are doing.

The day finally came when Miguel hit a career wall. He could no longer suppress his gut instincts. He had incredible support from his wife and kids, who absolutely adored him. It was time to knock down the wall and allow his personal and professional beings to come together as one. He wanted his identity back.

Are you sacrificing your beliefs in order to fit in?

Neglected

Have you ended up in a career or job where you no longer feel as though you have any control over how your office is run or your job performed? Do you feel as though you are drifting in the sea of corporate despair, neglected and shunted to the side by your boss? This warning sign is often the result of uncontrollable factors such as a management shake-up, corporate takeover, or the now-too-common bankruptcy. Now, you are struggling to make yourself relevant.

Marina, an extremely bright and talented financial controller, was in such a situation. Her career trajectory was unorthodox by most people's standards. Shortly after marriage, she stayed home to raise her kids and focus on building a home for her family. With her husband's ill health and eventual passing ten years later, she had to reenter the workforce in order to support her kids and provide for college.

Initially, Marina found success in a family-owned business close to where she lived. This afforded her an easy commute, flexibility, and a good salary with benefits. She was granted a lot of autonomy and latitude to manage her team. When the family business was sold, she was asked to stay on and work for the new owners. This seemed like a no-brainer for Marina. Until then, Marina had been spared the corporate politics that can cripple a person's spirit, but as the family owners left and the new owners came in, so did a new climate—like a cold wind from the north. While the new owners said they wanted her to stay on, she was feeling iced out. New processes and operating structures were being implemented without her knowledge. Many of these changes were not resonating with her. In fact, most of them she downright disagreed with. Her new boss, however, was prickly and not interested in what she had to say. He preferred her just to do what she was told. This was a hard pill to swallow.

This shift in her situation also led to a shift in her attitude. Her core personality traits, fun and easygoing, were supplanted by frustration and contempt. The problem fell squarely on her new boss. His lack of respect for her abilities and experience with the company were getting the best of her. So much so, she would lash out and challenge his decisions. Needless to say, this was not a healthy situation for Marina. She felt increasingly out of place and dispirited. This feeling was exacerbated as old coworkers were replaced with new ones. And the new ones were on board with the new owners and not interested in how things used to be. Over time, Marina's confidence began to erode, she felt more and more an outsider, neglected, pushed to the side, and unsure of her abilities. The impact on her psyche was significant. The lack of control and confidence sent her on a downward spiral. This led to more frequent outbursts and separation from the others. Her sphere of influence was minimized to a mere shadow of what it once was.

Has the relationship with your boss soured and your influence diminished?

Idling

Idling is characterized by the inability to make progress on decisions that affect you. You have become emotionally paralyzed and your life feels stuck. It begins when you lose sight of what you want and others become your focus. You put the wants and needs of others before yours. You feel the weight of every personal decision and the impact on those around you. So, you focus on others but there is a slow simmer that is happening inside. The frustration is mounting, and you feel like you are losing bits and pieces of yourself.

Danielle was a forty-three-year-old professional and mom of three girls, and she felt as though she were stuck in neutral. In her youth, she was full of energy and creativity. There was no limit to what she could do, especially with activities that made her feel fulfilled. She married her college sweetheart, and she worked for the same company for more than twenty years. A jubilant personality, Danielle would merrily go with the flow. At work, this involved moving throughout the company based solely on what management wanted her to do. When she started a family, she focused on building a home and strong support network to keep everyone safe and happy. This meant rushing home to tick items off the to-do list and shepherding the kids to their various activities.

Doing for others was slowly crowding out her needs and desires. Now, her life was centered on her three kids, her husband (whom she loved), and a demanding job. The guilt of being a working mom was significant. When she was not at work, she felt obligated to devote all her free time to being a mom and wife. The result was very little time to think about herself and what she wanted. For years, she was on autopilot. Although this seemed to work for a while, it was beginning to wear thin.

Danielle's selflessness became exacerbated when her employer began pressuring her to make a career decision that would force her to relinquish her ability to work from home two days a week. Her new boss wanted her in the office Monday through Friday. The decision required an examination of what she wanted to do, but she was paralyzed into inaction. Her inability to make decisions and move forward was crippling her spirit and limiting her job growth. She was a victim of her own internal dialogue regarding others' expectations of her.

What obligations are you imposing on yourself that are not allowing you to move forward?

No Focus

You might find yourself experiencing this warning sign if you enthusiastically imagine lots of potential career options but, like a kid in a candy store, can't quite decide which one you want. Ultimately, you are overwhelmed with all the choices and every day you come home with a new exciting possibility. While this is encouraging because you can see the opportunities, it is frustrating for you and those around you because there is a lot of talk and little action.

Anna was highly talented, with a track record of success. Fifteen years into her career, she had held numerous positions within her company and was well regarded by senior management. Through a series of promotions and job changes, she landed a management position with significant responsibilities. However, she did not feel particularly fulfilled. She didn't necessarily like being in management. It took away from the actual delivery of the product to the consumer, and the position was riddled with political sensitivities that constantly had to be addressed. After the sheen of the new title wore off, her job enjoyment level was waning fast and this led to professional reflection. She questioned whether her current company was the best fit and began to entertain other career options.

A hard look at the state of her current career caused Anna to seek out other opportunities. Given her wide interests and capabilities, she cast a wide net. Anyone who showed interest in her skill, as well as companies that had always piqued her curiosity, influenced her decisions. Each day she would come home with a new idea. As Anna became more restless for change, the ideas began to vary widely. While her family was supportive, the constant merry-go-round of ideas was exhausting. After a while, her husband no longer knew how to respond. He was becoming concerned, as the considerations potentially involved moving and there was a significant shift away from the work she had always loved doing.

Anna's head was spinning, and she was feeling really unsettled. She did not have a filter for how to make decisions. She was afraid to say no to anything for fear of losing out on an opportunity, but at the same time, she was not willing to commit without a clearer vision. This led to professional and personal swirl. Over time, it was draining her emotional energy and handicapping her performance at work.

She was squandering her talent and not maximizing her current or potential opportunities. Anna was in desperate need of focus.

Are you overwhelmed by what is possible and in professional swirl?

Growing Discontent

By all accounts you have a great job. The title. The money. The office. The prestige of working for a respected company. But still, you are not feeling fulfilled, and it's wearing you down. During your ascent through the company, you collected all the trinkets of success, but you lost sight of what really gets you excited. Now you know what you want to be doing, but you haven't yet found the path forward. Something or someone is holding you back.

Patrick knew what he wanted to do for a living as soon as he got to college. His dedication showed. He built a vibrant career and was spotted as someone capable of sitting on the executive floor. His group operated as a finely tuned machine, and he garnered the respect of his team and upper management. By all accounts he was on the right path. There was just one issue: Patrick was not doing what really inspired him. He could see what inspired him; it was just across the hall in another office. However, because of the great work and value that Patrick was bringing to his current position, the company was hesitant for him to expand or change his role.

Up to this point, Patrick had resigned himself to his post. Although there were times when he wanted to make a change, he had been placated by the salary, bonus, and expense accounts that came with his position. It was doable. Once the novelty of the perks and prestige began to wear off, however, the satisfaction of a job well done was not enough to keep him motivated. He was left with an odd sense of disenchantment with his position, the company, and his boss. This was beginning to spill over into all aspects of his life. In fact, it made him begin to take stock of where else he lacked fulfillment.

In some respects, he was fighting battles that he did not sign up for. Over the years, he had proven himself adept at putting out fires and righting other people's problems. While he was good at it, and it was valuable to the company, Patrick was not inspired to continue down this path. He wanted to shift from the role of cleanup to being more strategic in setting the course for the future. Patrick saw a future where better up-front thinking and leading would result in more prosperity and less need for cleanup. He saw the same mistakes being made over and over and knew the corrections he made could be instituted systematically across the company. Yet, when he brought it up with management, he was told, "Just keep doing what you're doing." He began to feel he was banging his head against a wall, and he was no longer garnering much fulfillment from his career.

The tricky part for Patrick was that a change for him would not necessarily be seen as a valuable change for his company. They valued the work he was doing. A change might mean leaving the company. He needed a plan and unwavering commitment to make it happen.

Is your company holding you back from moving your career forward?

What the Seven W.A.R.N.I.N.G. Signs Have in Common

Three threads weave through all seven W.A.R.N.I.N.G. Signs of Distress. Identifying these threads will help you get to the root of the problem and enable you to craft a new vision for yourself.

Relinquishing control of one's life

When you relinquish control of your life, you find yourself in a position of waiting for someone else to make decisions on your behalf. This can happen if you're overwhelmed and unsure of what action to take. The result is inaction. This can also happen if you're deferring decisions about your career to others. The result is reaction. Take Danielle, who is Idling. She has gotten so caught up in the agenda of her employer and family that she has lost sight of her own goals and desires. In the past, she followed the lead of others and trusted that they had her best interests in mind. It wasn't until the confluence of events that she realized how much of her decision-making authority she had relinquished to others. She was giving too much credence to the opinion of others and giving in to what they were saying. She wasn't effectively balancing others' beliefs with her own. She lost touch with what is truly important for her and therefore was drifting.

I see this often with clients who have successfully been on career autopilot. It's usually those who have been at the same company for a long time, where their career decisions are heavily influenced by management. They have cultivated a satisfying career based on the decisions of others.

Life is running smoothly until there is an event such as management or business upheaval. When faced with a new reality that requires them to make decisions on their own behalf, they become paralyzed, usually because they have never had to answer the question "What do you want to do?" It's shocking to me—people take on tremendous responsibilities within their organizations or family, but take little responsibility for their career or life.

Putting the needs, wants, and desires of others before one's own, either at work, at home, or both

This is significant especially in dual-income families in which parents are saddled with guilt for not being home with the kids as much as they think they should. Women tend to be more affected with guilt because they are more aware of their feelings. I remember at family dinners as a kid, my mom always took her food last, and if something was burnt it ended up on her plate. I see it at the office. Certain people are always looking out for and helping others. While this may give you a momentary sense of joy, over time it has the good chance of turning into resentment.

Recently I spoke with a friend who has been working at a family-owned company for more than twenty years. He has been there from the beginning. Over the years, he has been a loyal and faithful employee. Because of his connection to the family, he would go over and above and make himself available 24/7. And while he was well compensated, he would put the company first, whether that meant picking up the slack of others, taking on additional responsibilities, or forgoing his free time with his family to cater to any urgent request. Over time, this was not sitting well, especially when he began to feel a lack of respect for his time and capabilities. The feelings of resentment were bubbling up. All the needs of the company and its owners were being met, but not his. As predicted, it came to a head, and a tough but warranted conversation took place. While it is hard to change twenty years of a specific pattern, progress can be made to ensure both parties' needs are met at the same level. In this situation, you have to be especially careful if someone else has more to gain by you doing what they want.

Losing belief in oneself

A lack of belief in yourself is a great example of putting too much stock in what others have to say about you and your skills. This happens often in highly competitive businesses. It is easy to lose your mojo if people are casting doubt on your abilities. And if your self-confidence is a bit fragile, you can end up believing the critics. When a client is being confronted with criticism, I ask him or her to look at the feedback from two perspectives: Is it personal or is it situational?

It is personal if in your heart you believe it to be true. Maybe you did not give your best on an assignment. Maybe you have taken on more than you can handle and you are overwhelmed. Maybe you are in a job that is not really interesting to you. These are instances where you are culpable for the outcome.

It is situational when external forces are what make your success a challenge. This could be because of a boss who is overly critical, condescending, and brusque. If management is treating everyone this way, you should not be taking it personally. If the culture is such that nothing is ever good enough, then you can accept it as the norm and proceed accordingly.

Too often I have clients who are trying to decipher situations and people in order to determine what is personal and what is situational.

When something is being taken as personal, I can see the anguish in the person's face. People put a lot of effort into their jobs and want to succeed, and it's easy to take criticism as a personal attack. As the coach, I help decipher the situation and give it some perspective. This is especially helpful for those who are at a new company or have a new boss. Different companies and bosses have their own code for how they work and interact with others. You could have a boss who is a yeller, but he or she yells at everyone. You may work for a company or on a team where everyone constantly teases or ribs each other. Developing your own set of core beliefs will help you decide if this is okay with you and fend off being victim to others' whims.

Moving forward and breaking your current cycle takes guts and perseverance. You have to cultivate a belief within yourself that thriving is the only option. Accountability is key at that stage. You have to own up and resist the temptation to blame it on others. The more responsibility you take for your life, the more reward, at any age.

What Is the State of Your Life?

Which way is your life arc trending? If you find it is on a downward trajectory, your career, quite possibly, is playing a significant role in your unhappiness. However, other factors may also be contributing to your current state of dismay. Yes, your career is important to your life, but maybe not in the way it once was. What motivated you in the past may be different now and into the future. If you are going to make a positive change, it is important to understand and recalibrate your life given where you are today and what you have learned over time.

So, when was the last time you thought about you and your life holistically? It would not be unusual to say "never." Yet, stepping back to take a fresh look at your life can be quite illuminating. Whether you know it or not, certain aspects of your life have greater influence on your well-being than others. Most likely, you are not conscious of these positive and negative influences because you're living your daily routine without much thought. Although you may be able to sense when your career or personal life is in trouble, you may not be able to identify what exactly is off-kilter.

To move forward, you must assess where you are today and uncover the problem areas. You have to be honest in answering the question "How do I really feel?" To do this, you need to be present and open. The focus will be on what you can control. The Life Line Assessment is a great tool to get you started. This simple self-assessment features ten dimensions separated into three core areas:

· How I make a living: career and finances
· How I treat myself: health, personal growth, personal/physical environment, and spirituality
· How I treat others: friends and family, fun and recreation, significant other/romance, and community

The completed Life Line Assessment visually depicts the current state of your life. For most, it's a great exercise to ground them in where their life is today. This is a tough exercise because our lives are so intertwined with others. You may have lost sight of your personal motivators versus those that come along with your job or spouse. It also is not easy to see what is important when you are busy living life, and your view of life can quickly become distorted. Some people are shocked to discover how off-kilter their life has become. Or how sensitive they are to certain aspects of their life. Often the aspects of your life that you view as "frivolous" are squeezed out, and yet many of these supposedly frivolous activities give you joy and energy. Quite possibly you will uncover several areas that need attention.

When you take an outside view of things, you may realize you have been putting too much emphasis on fixing your career when in reality you will achieve more when you create more meaningful relationships with others. Assessing your life in totality will bring a new, eye-opening perspective. A happy, satisfying life is never one- or even two-dimensional.

John's Story

John was particularly concerned about his career. His company was downsizing and moving its headquarters. He did not want to move and was now faced with the prospect of finding a new job. When he completed his Life Line Assessment, it was not surprising to see that his career and money scored low. What did surprise John was how low he rated his health. Quite frankly, he had not thought much about his health for a long time. In his twenties, he was very active and played various sports. At the time, he was quite proud of his physique. Once he became involved in a relationship, his level of physical activity began to diminish and his eating habits changed. It was not a priority for the relationship, so he stopped playing sports. He and his partner were more inclined to go out to eat and socialize with friends and family. He knew that he had put on a few pounds and was more likely to choose the couch over the gym, but what he did not realize was how much he missed the physicality and camaraderie of playing sports.

Between his career and relationship, it was hard to find the time to work out. While initially John was disappointed that he had let such an important part of his life completely slip away, he realized that this was a perfect opportunity to make it a priority again. With the impending change in his career, he decided to make sure that this was a factor in choosing a job. If he could cut down on his commute time, he would have more time to dedicate to himself. He also broached this topic with his partner. And while his partner didn't have a keen interest in joining him in his athletic pursuits, she did realize that it was important and she supported him. ✍

As you work through the Life Line Assessment, you may add to or subtract from the definition of each dimension. If that helps make it your own and create relevance, please go ahead. These dimensions should feel real to you. It's most important to look for the truths and how these influence your life today and what you want to take action on in the future. Once you have completed the assessment, you will formulate a plan to move forward.

THE LIFE LINE ASSESSMENT

Directions

Using a scale of 1 to 10, with 10 being the most satisfied, rate your satisfaction with each area of your life. Answer each question individually and then average your score for each dimension. To find the average, add up your scores, then divide by the number of items in the dimension. Use the chart at the end of this section to track your scores and create a visual depiction of your life line.

How You Make a Living

This is core for most people since making money affects a person's standard of living. You spend a significant portion of your day working, either at a place of employment or taking care of the home and family. Take care to assess where you are today, rather than where you have been in the past or where you think you should be.

CAREER

___ I have a fulfilling career where my talents and skills are well utilized

___ I enjoy my work environment and the people with whom I work

___ I see a career path of growth and opportunity

___ I enjoy going to work and have energy at the end of the day

___ Average score

FINANCES

___ I am satisfied with my current income level

___ I manage my money and financial affairs well

___ I am free of constant financial worry and stress about money

___ My financial future feels sustainable

___ Average score

How You Treat Yourself

Not surprisingly, taking care of yourself can be relegated to the back burner. And yet, it is essential to longevity. The healthier you are correlates to how much you can realize your vision. If your body and mind are not functioning at full capacity, you will not be able to fully move forward. This includes having a place where you can recharge and draw energy.

HEALTH

__ I feel good about the way I look

__ I am in great shape and take responsibility to exercise regularly and eat well

__ I am proactive in my approach to health

__ I have a support network in place that allows me to easily maintain my health and well-being

__ Average score

PERSONAL GROWTH

__ I am living the life I want

__ I am evolving and growing as an individual

__ I regularly engage in activities and learning that excite me

__ I approach life as a series of adventures to experience

__ Average score

PERSONAL AND PHYSICAL ENVIRONMENT

__ I love my home, its surroundings, and being there

__ The level of order in my surroundings is appropriate to my needs

__ My wardrobe expresses my style and I love the clothes I wear

__ Average score

SPIRITUALITY

__ I regularly attend a place of worship

__ I believe in a higher being

__ I live a religious life

__ Average score

How You Treat Others

Demanding careers and long commutes can easily consume most of your day. Therefore, the amount of time you spend with others as well as how you treat them can be jeopardized.

FRIENDS AND FAMILY

__ I am close to my family and circle of friends

__ I enjoy being with my family and circle of friends

__ I trust the relationships I have with my family and friends

__ I am energized by my relationships

__ Average score

FUN AND RECREATION

__ I regularly take the time to experience play, adventure, and leisure

__ I know what activities renew and energize me, and I participate in them regularly

__ I create plenty of space in my life to relax and enjoy time with others

__ I have fun

__ Average score

SIGNIFICANT OTHER/ROMANCE

__ I am satisfied and content with my current situation, either my relationship with a partner or being single

__ I feel loved by the people who mean the most to me

__ I am open to creating an intimate, loving relationship

__ I create romance in my life

__ Average score

COMMUNITY

__ I engage in activities that help others

__ I volunteer my time at local organizations

__ I am actively involved in neighborhood activities

__ Average score

YOUR LIFE LINE ASSESSMENT SCORES

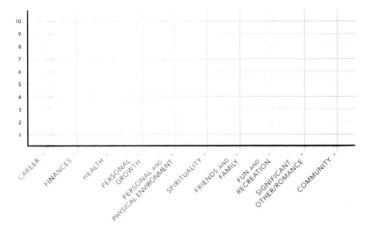

How did you do? What does your life line look like? How closely does your life line represent how you feel? Is it pretty flat and consistent? Or are there peaks and valleys? What picture does it paint? Which areas are solid, a 7 or above? Which areas are okay, 4–7? Which areas need some attention, below a 4? Now rank them in order of importance for you to address. It would be overwhelming and impossible to address all of them. By prioritizing them, you will have focus.

Remember, there is no right answer, but your response to this assessment should illuminate where to create a plan of action and where you can look for inspiration. For example, say you are an 8 in Friends and Family and a 4 in Health. Is there a way to improve your health by marrying it with family and friends? One of my clients relishes time spent with his friends. To help improve his health, they agreed to work out together. This way they can hang out together and get in shape.

Another client of mine realized the importance of environment for her. Her surroundings had a direct impact on how she felt. While this had always been the case, it wasn't something that she really internalized, nor did she realize the impact it had on everything else until she completed the Life Line Assessment. Her home and her surroundings bring her much joy and happiness. Having a home that is warm, comfortable, and organized brings an immediate calmness when she walks in the door. Being in her space provides a sanctuary where she can unwind. This became complicated once she was married with a child and had another on the way. Her space was now their space. Husband plus children doesn't always make for a calm sanctuary. This had a cascading effect on her relationship and career. She found herself more and more on edge. A big part of this was not the relationship with her husband or her job. It was that she did not have a place to go where she could recharge. She realized she needed a space that was all her own. As she probed this in further detail, she uncovered how much environment motivates her and her comfort level. By bringing attention to this she was clear about what environments were most energizing. In particular, too much visual noise wore her down. When it was chaotic and there was stuff everywhere, she shut down. Just uncovering this insight has made it easier for her to handle unpleasant environments. She knows visual chaos is a trigger. Rather than letting the circumstance frustrate her, thanks to the Life Line Assessment she can at least understand why she feels the way she does and figure out how she can best deal with it.

≡ KEY QUESTIONS ≈≈≈≈≈≈≈≈≈≈≈≈≈≈≈≈≈≈≈≈≈≈≈≈≈

- How would you describe your current situation?
- Are you feeling boxed in?
- What's your warning sign?
- What does your life line look like?

It's Never Too Late to Reinvent Your Career

There is a prevailing sentiment that once past age forty, you're too old to change career paths. The transition is too risky. You have too many responsibilities, and you may put your reputation in jeopardy. Taking chances is for the young. Besides, reinventing yourself means starting over. And starting over is daunting.

I definitely don't believe that to be true. You should not confuse reinvention with starting over. Case in point: Phyllis Diller, who in 2013 passed away at the age of ninety-five. Diller had a career writing advertising copy for a radio station. At the age of forty, with a brood of five kids, she wrote her last copy line and turned to comedy. She reinvented her career while raising her family and being the primary breadwinner. She didn't know exactly how she was going to do it. There was no road map to follow, but she was taking control. And by all accounts she never looked back. It was a risky time for a female comedian to be out on the circuit doing a solo act. All the others were part of a male/female act; most famous at the time was Gracie Allen, who played dumb to George Burns.

Not only did she burst onto the scene at the age of forty, her comedic career spanned more than forty years as she performed well into her eighties. So, what can we learn from Phyllis Diller? Here are a few pointers on how to reinvent your career, gleaned from her life:

· **Take control.** Phyllis Diller took control and leveraged her strengths. As an advertising writer she was adept at creating humorous headlines. At the same time, she was cultivating a local audience that marveled at her humorous stories. She turned her focus to crafting and delivering rapid-fire one-liners. This served as the centerpiece of her act.

· **Do what you love and don't be afraid of filling your own needs.** Making people laugh is what she loved doing. This meant being selfish with her dream while still raising a family. What would have happened if she had only considered the needs and wants of her family? Instead, she gathered the support of her husband as well as a cadre of other like-minded comedians breaking through at that time.

· **Follow your convictions.** Diller had such inner belief and conviction. I love the fact that she made her stand-up her own. She created a unique persona around being the anti-housewife, wearing wacky outfits, and bellowing her trademark laugh.

Think of what we would have missed had Phyllis Diller thought she was too old to reinvent her career. Make no mistake, reinventing your career is hard work. Phyllis Diller was fond of saying that she ordered a bucket of guts every morning. But you could tell that she loved what she was doing.

A smile is a curve that sets everything straight.
—PHYLLIS DILLER (ATTRIBUTED)

STEP TWO

FORMULATING YOUR PLAN
TO AMPLIFY YOUR LIFE

CHAPTER FOUR

WHAT'S YOUR REALITY?

During the final years of my advertising career, I was selected to participate in a leadership study focusing on resilience. This included a series of
mini breakout sessions where we debriefed our individual survey results
with each other. We were asked to share with our breakout group what
we were most proud of as it related to our career. Two people in my
group said, "Surviving." In the past, I would have glossed over such a
comment because it is commonplace. How many times do we say or
hear, "I survived . . . " However, this time, I started to listen closely to how
they were talking about surviving. For one participant, it was surviving
over thirty years with the same company. While others had come and
gone, she had endured just about every imaginable business challenge,
management incarnation, and personal situation. Her goal was to keep
moving away from assignments, people, and situations that were unpleasant. She created a protective fortress around herself and spent enormous
amounts of energy to guard what she had. Surviving for her equaled
self-preservation.

For the other, it was surviving what he considered to be the bureau-
cracy and "stupidity" of everyone else. In his mind, every day he had to
do battle against the politics and the corporate machine. He believed
that it was a war of attrition; he would survive by continuing to drive

home his point of view until someone else broke. It was as if he wielded a giant battering ram, and he would continue to apply enough force to break through.

This survival mentality allowed them both to have sustaining and relatively successful careers; however, both also had incredible amounts of bitterness and resentment toward their company and their colleagues. Neither spoke of being particularly fulfilled, engaged, or challenged. In fact, both spoke of how they would "survive" until retirement.

I sat there wondering how people can live like that day after day. Quite frankly, I do not think they even saw it in themselves. It had become such ingrained behavior. The speech pattern was always the same. The villains were always the same. It was always someone else's fault. Survivors talk in terms of what others are not allowing them to do or be. "I cannot do my job because other people are getting in my way." As these two partici- pants were talking, I was feeling more and more weighed down by their heaviness. I was beginning to feel depressed by the realization that this is how a lot of people feel about their job. I could not imagine spending the majority of my life feeling satisfied with having survived. Realizing that longevity is not a viable career strategy, I walked out of the conference room emboldened not to end up the same way. It was time for me to take a stand and answer the question "What do I want?" I do not want my badge of honor to be that I survived. I want to thrive. How about you?

To thrive is to prosper. To thrive is to grow and develop vigorously. To thrive is to be fortunate and successful. To thrive is to be clear about what you really want. Inherent in thriving is a readiness for action that will result in change. You have reached readiness when the status quo is no longer acceptable. To achieve change, you must be motivated and committed.

I hear a lot of clients lament that in order to do what they want to do, they would have to take steps that will negatively impact their life and family, especially their financial security. "If I like what I do, I will make less money" is their stance. "Therefore, I will stick with an unpleasant work situation that pays well so I can provide for my family." For some, the mind-set is that it is work; the point is to make money to provide for your family. It is not supposed to be enjoyable. It is a twisted thought process of misery equals financial and job security. If the recent tough years have taught us anything, it is that there is no "safe" job. In that light, you have to be clear about what you want to do and keep pushing toward that end.

In fairness, I can understand and empathize with why people go into survival mode at work and, for some, in life. It can be unnerving to be out there swinging from the branches. And if you are somewhat risk averse you want guarantees. "Of course I want to thrive and do what I want to do, but . . ." The one word that keeps us locked in survival mode is "but." This simple little three-letter word can be a powerful deterrent to your being able to move to a thriving life.

Not long ago, I was working with a client who wanted to make a change in her life. After twenty years in corporate America, she wanted to start her own business. She was tired of the office politics and having her ideas squelched by others. She wanted to create something that utilized her strengths and would allow for greater personal fulfillment. Needless to say, I was very excited about the prospect of helping her move toward her goal.

As we began to work together, there were two themes emerging that were keeping her in survival mode. The first was mitigating all financial risk. I can completely understand the desire to protect your financial assets. It can be scary to put your hard-earned money on the line without a guarantee of positive returns. However, there are no guarantees or absolutes in anything. Even if you are gainfully employed now, you are not assured of a job tomorrow. And while there are some pretty good predictors that things will be the same day after day, even those will change and evolve.

The second theme was the use of the word *but*. Whenever our discussion turned to the possibilities of a new future, it quickly began to devolve downward, as she consistently used the word *but* to shoot down any ideas that would move her toward her goal. This became a powerfully creative survival tool. There were always extremely well thought out reasons why she couldn't possibly pursue her dream. At the end of each conversation was a long list of *buts*.

What I found is that it was oddly comforting to dream about what could be *but*—look, I just used it—not put ourselves out there to make it a reality. While it is "safe" to keep the status quo, it is frustrating to have aspirations of a life that would make you thrive only to have it thwarted by *but*.

By living a life focused on surviving, you are giving away so much of your own power and surrendering your ability to thrive. I am not advocating that everyone quits his or her job tomorrow. I am advocating that you can change the arc of your life and move forward toward what you want. This will positively impact not only you but also those in your life.

Sarah's Story

Sarah was feeling less than satisfied with her career. After years of being self-confident and upbeat she had begun to feel overwhelmed and cornered. Even with sixteen years under her belt, she doubted herself and looked to others for approval. This resulted in her inability to proactively move projects along. Part of it was a new company and new colleagues who thrived on instilling fear and doubt in others. Another part of it was that she was allowing herself to be swayed by others. Her work life was impacting her personal life. She was becoming increasingly moody and looking for an escape route: "I need to find a new job." "We need to move." "Maybe I need to go back to school." It was affecting her home life and frustrating her family. Eventually, she realized she had allowed others to take the fun out of her job and her life. She was becoming increasingly disenfranchised with everything. At the core, she knew that she was questioning her abilities because of her pedigree, or lack thereof. She was more street smart than book smart. Tired of being scared, she took back her life. No longer would she cower to others. This meant bringing forward the best of her and what she had to offer. The result was more fun, more courage to express her point of view, and more self-confidence. The impact was a promotion and stronger relationships with colleagues, not to mention a husband who has witnessed a marked change. Today, she is more present, active, and settled. No longer is she being reactive. She has developed a plan for how she wants to move forward.

The impact was not only evident at work. Her husband remarked how he felt his wife of years ago has returned. Unfortunately, it was true that her work life impacted her personal life and her personal life impacted her work life. The frustration and self-doubt she felt at work is no longer finding its way into her personal life. Her joy of life has been recaptured. She is more engaged, relaxed, and happy at home. This includes training for triathlons with her husband and having fun playing with her daughter. The change is noticeable and, most important, she feels great about herself. No more self-doubt. ᪣

Sometimes a decision to do what you want may involve taking a lower salary, learning a new industry, or going back to school—a short-term solution for long-term gains and enhanced career gratification. It may also mean resetting your attitude and approach to your current job and how you want to be. In either case, it involves discussions with your family and assessment of whether a better quality of life is more important that a certain standard of living. I have a client who downsized their home and standard of living knowing that a future career change may result in lower compensation. The family has easily adapted to this new lifestyle, realizing they didn't need a bigger house filled with lots of stuff. And it has eliminated the pressure of holding on to a job in order to survive, thus creating more room in order to thrive.

What Does It Mean to Move Forward?

First and foremost, you must have a desire to let go of the past. As you age and grow wiser, you also accumulate a lot of disappointments and points of pain. These tend to crowd out your accomplishments and periods of happiness. This is especially true if you do not have a vision for your life. Without a vision, you allow your past to define your future. And like many people, you may have allowed the past to happen to you. Success is defined by how well you can maneuver around each new obstacle that has been placed before you. This requires an incredible amount of energy and associated feelings of angst. Over time, it can be mentally and physically taxing to know that every day you are merely bracing for survival.

Moving forward not only requires a vision but also the acceptance that the past is not an indication of the future. To enact a vision, you must have motivation and commitment.

What does it mean to be motivated and committed? There are countless times when you are motivated to take on a new challenge (begin exercising, start a new hobby, take on a home improvement project). In the beginning, you are ambitious and pour a lot of energy into this new challenge. You excitedly join a health club, buy fruits and vegetables, and purchase a new pair of running shoes. During this honeymoon phase, you make it a priority and carve out time in your day. You talk about it liberally with family, friends, and colleagues. But then your interest begins to wane; it becomes more challenging than you thought. You easily become preoccupied with other distractions. The initial burst of energy is down to a flicker. Before you know it, this new challenge begins to collect dust in the corner, never to be touched again. The missing piece was commitment.

For Linda, a client of mine, her challenge was to live a healthier life by losing weight—no small task for someone who had waged a lifelong battle. Recent health issues heightened the urgency to take action. From the beginning, she understood that motivation would only get her started. Commitment would be essential to her conquering this challenge.

We started by establishing a visual goal that had two core elements: how she wanted to see herself and a time frame for success. Immediately, she zeroed in on fitting into her wedding dress before her twentieth anniversary, nine months away, quite an aggressive time frame. She took a mental snapshot of what she would look like and how she would feel. This became permanently etched in her brain. In addition to her visual goal, she focused on defining her values and crafting a purpose. Having a visual goal, values, and a purpose created a core belief system that would anchor her and her commitment to this challenge. She needed this solid support structure to withstand the inevitable waning of motivation she knew would kick in. This was not the first time she had tried to get healthy.

She also knew that enlisting the help and resources of others was critical. This was no journey to take alone. Initially, she had great success in losing weight and keeping it off. High-fives and soaring motivation abounded. True to form, however, the initial buzz of adrenaline dissipated over time and the true test of her resolve happened during the middle stretch, when progress was slow. She stayed committed by constantly referencing and honoring her visual goal, values, and purpose. Through all the temptation, frustration, and low points where doubts crept in, she pulled herself out. She was severely tested, but she never waivered. This time she was in control of herself and how she would respond.

She lost sixty-five pounds (and counting) and successfully integrated healthy eating into her life. As a reward, she treated herself to a new wardrobe bought at a store she used to bypass. People are constantly commenting on how she looks. While this does wonders for her self-esteem, she is disappointed that people cannot see the inside, because that is where she really feels the change. She is living her best self on the inside and outside.

Oh yeah, and the wedding dress? It was too big. So what is next? For the outside—improved fitness and tone. For the inside—acceptance of how she looks.

Developing Your Dynamic Goals

Now it's your turn to set goals based on the areas of your life you want to amplify. Not surprisingly, this is the one thing everyone says they will do and yet most people do not.

Many of us are reluctant to write down and commit to goals. The prospect of success is overshadowed by the fear of failure. I can empathize;

I used to feel that way. I never wanted to let myself down if I did not accomplish a goal. This meant I was a bit rudderless. I had a vague idea of where I was headed, but it was just that—vague. I was afraid to make my plan concrete. When I decided to change careers, I knew that I would have to rely on my inner drive in order to achieve success. This meant being more rigorous with my goals. My goals now play an important role in my decision-making process. I am better at how and where I focus my effort and time. It also alleviates any doubt that I might be wasting my time. I will always choose to spend my time doing activities that will help me achieve my goals.

Dynamic Goals should stretch you out of your comfort zone. They should break up your routine. Remember, it is about embracing change in order to thrive. Change can be difficult to do on your own, but achieving your goals doesn't have to be a solo effort. Enlist others to help you. Sometimes you can even bring others along on your journey. I had a client with a goal of living a healthier life. This meant better eating habits and exercise. While she specifically subscribed to Weight Watchers (enlisting the help of others) she wanted to bring better eating habits to her family too. She did this through buying less processed and packaged food and more fruits and vegetables so that fruits and vegetables played a more prominent role in their meals. She never declared that the family would start eating healthy; she just started doing it. Over time, the entire family was eating healthier and losing weight. Now packaged food is an exception versus a staple.

In 2011, I completed my second year of defining and living my goals. I was surprised to learn how the very act of articulating and committing my goals to paper cleared space for most of them to be realized. But I did have an interesting experience.

During the holidays, I was at a cocktail party chatting with some friends. I was ruminating and somewhat gloating about how I achieved all my goals. There I was, standing tall and feeling quite proud of my accomplishments. During the course of the year, I had successfully navigated the transition from corporate employee to entrepreneur. With perseverance and hard work, I launched a coaching program for my past employer, where I now serve as an outside consultant, as well as building my own coaching practice. I was involved in two significant not-for-profit initiatives and successfully sold our family home of fifty-six years (in a Detroit suburb, no less).

So, there I was, sporting a broad, boastful smile when I was greeted with "Well, maybe you did not set your goals high enough." I nearly passed out. What? I did not set my goals high enough? Are you kidding me? And they were not. They were serious—not malicious or condescending, just serious. And I was tongue-tied. Then I went into full coach mode, explaining why these goal achievements were significant and worthy of a little bragging. To my surprise, I did not recoil. I was not going to let someone else rain on my goal parade. I achieved them and I was going to stand tall in my accomplishments.

But it did make me stop to wonder. How do we set our goals? How much do we push for the unattainable? For me, historically, I would underpromise and overdeliver. But could I have overdelivered even more? I decided to chill out and take a different perspective about goal setting and achievement. In recent years, I've become more vigilant in setting goals and I realize their importance. I also recognize I have to stretch myself. Each year I push the limits further to see the potential upside. I do not always hit every goal on time or in the way I had intended. I had wanted to start my own business a year earlier. In retrospect, however, patience proved to be my greatest ally (I'll talk more about patience later), and the achievement of my goals was something to be proud of.

Whether you receive positive affirmation from others or not, you need to recognize and value your accomplishments. There will always be something that didn't get done or that was not completed to the perfect standards you set. That shouldn't deter you from patting yourself on the back and reveling in your success.

Let us get you on track. At this point, it is important to prioritize, or else you will be overwhelmed or become the victim of the overly ambitious syndrome. This happens when your eagerness for change is actually more than you can handle at one time. Changing your arc takes time and patience and cannot be accomplished in one fell swoop. Now that you know what areas to focus on, based on your Life Line Assessment, the next step is to set Dynamic Goals that have a time horizon of 0 to 24 months. This may seem like a short time frame, but I have found that people are more likely to take action against goals that have a payoff in the near future.

Dynamic Goals are designed to put you in motion. They should be goals that you can accomplish quickly with noticeable results. Success comes from effective action. These small wins will create forward momentum that you can build upon. The sense of accomplishment will become addictive, and you will be looking forward to tackling the next one on the list. These short bursts of activity will ignite your fire and manifest into something big and beautiful. Your achievement of these Dynamic Goals will perpetuate stability. Having a foundation to build upon will generate confidence as you tackle each goal. More important, you will be energized and excited about re-creating the process and witnessing firsthand the changes you can make in your life.

In this exercise you will create three sets of Dynamic Goals, short term (0–6 months), medium term (6–18 months), and long term (18–24 months). Generally speaking, your short-term and medium-term goals will include those steps that help put you in position to achieve your long-term goals. As you formulate your list, follow these guidelines:

- Write down each goal and be specific. The more specific and measurable the goals are, the easier it is to take action.
- Have a mix of goals that are internally focused, such as personal growth, and externally focused, such as improving friendships.
- Make sure you have some fun goals on your list. Life is to be enjoyed.
- Put the list in a visible place and cross off your goals once completed. Then, take the time to celebrate each accomplishment.

One example of a long-term Dynamic Goal may be to get promoted to vice president within the next two years. That in itself is quite admirable but also could be overwhelming. To make it manageable, you will need to outline a series of smaller, tangible accomplishments that will put you in the ideal position for that promotion. Are there opportunities to expand your current responsibilities with assignments that will be part of a VP's role? Are there projects that will allow you to interact with key influencers within the organization who will have a voice when it comes time to select the next class of VPs? Are there leadership skills that you need to further develop that will be required of people at that level? The accomplishment of these short- or medium-term Dynamic Goals will put you in the best position to achieve your long-term goal.

Here are a few more examples:

Short term

Beginning today, I will improve the quality of the time I spend with my family by keeping my electronic devices out of sight when we are together during the evening and on the weekend.

Medium term

I will attend at least one networking event every quarter with the expressed intent of meeting at least three new people and expanding my contacts.

Long term

I will be in a position where I can have more control over my career and my future, and that allows me the time and resources to ensure my life includes a gratifying career along with activities that keep me healthy.

Creating Space to Achieve Your Goals

Setting goals is an important step for changing the arc of your life. However, to achieve those goals, you have to create space in your life. As I noted earlier in the book, our lives have become crowded with demands and obligations. You may have spent many years gathering and holding on to wants and needs that you thought were critical to your life. You may be saying to yourself, "I want and need the next promotion. I want and need a bigger house. I want and need more stuff." When you are making changes, you have to be open to cutting out at least some of these wants and needs.

In my own life, I spent years striving for the next promotion. I was doing everything I needed to get that coveted title, status, and associated perks. However, it wasn't turning out as planned, and I was beyond frustrated. I created massive amounts of internal strife for myself. When I began to realize that my career was headed in a new and different direction, it became evident that in order to create space for the new, I had to let go of the old. That also meant accepting the unachieved—accepting that I was not going to achieve something I set out to do, something I had invested time and energy in. This was not easy. And while I knew where I was now headed would be rewarding and fulfilling, I still had this nagging sense of defeat. People would know—and I would know—that I just did not get there.

Interestingly enough, once I finally let go and freed that mental space, I began to feel lighter and less encumbered. I did have to mourn the loss of the unachieved, but once I did, it was as if a weight had been lifted from my shoulders. I freed myself from something that ultimately was not that important to me: I realized I wanted the promotion because it was there, not because it would make my life more fulfilled.

Letting go not only frees up mental space but it also has an impact on your physical well-being. As you hold on to too many things that are not meaningful, you create stress in your body and life. It can manifest itself in many ways, and as you get older, it can worsen because your body naturally begins to break down (sad but true). This stress has a compounding effect that can cause irreparable harm if you do not address it early. As I shed the things that were not serving me, it became evident in how I look: More people commented on how "different" I look than ever before. And more than that, I stand up straighter, seem more relaxed, and feel happy. I am less burdened emotionally and physically.

Opening Up to Change

All this sounds great, but letting go is not easy. For most, it is downright terrifying. Life's journey is filled with ups and downs, joy and disappointment. With age, the downs and disappointments tend to weigh heavily and squash your spirit. As a guard against further disappointments, you may develop a protective armor that entrenches you in your comfort zone. This armor does an incredible job of keeping you safe from further disappointments. It also keeps out any substantial upside. It protects you by maintaining the status quo. When you consider stepping outside your comfort zone, there is concern that the status quo will be disrupted. The warning signals start firing. The brain is flooded with images and messages of failure and disappointment. "This is not going to turn out as planned," your brain tells you. "Remember what happened last time."

As adults, our comfort zone gets smaller and the wall around the perimeter taller. It is easier to justify saying no rather than saying yes. Saying no means you keep the status quo in check. The status quo is filled with "safe" activities. No pain. No disappointment. No upside. No downside. This includes not even entertaining other possibilities or actions. They get shot down immediately. Excuses fill the air and justify why things need to stay the way they are. You are protecting yourself from harm. You are also missing out on a lot of new and different experiences.

How can you begin to break through this armor? The best way to reinforce positive change is with some small victories. This is when you must look to your Dynamic Goals. With each goal you cross off the list, your comfort zone expands and your natural inclination to play it safe diminishes. You are slowly making room for change.

I have always been faithful about going to the gym and working out. I have never really been very keen on running, however. In fact, it is fair to say I really do not find much enjoyment from lacing up my running shoes and hitting the pavement. That being said, I decided to add running to my workout regimen as a way to improve my endurance and overall health and to increase my time outside. I started during the summer with a very modest one-mile run. Since I was doing this just for me, I did not care how fast I went or what I looked like. It was also critical for me not to get overzealous and set my sights too high. I decided to run two times a week and add distance as was comfortable. In the past, I had lost interest quickly, and I was prepared for the same to happen this time. Surprisingly, I found enjoyment in running twice a week. I built on small victories and slowly increased my distance. I now run a 5k twice a week. For me, running twice a week fits perfectly into my life. Each time I go out, I enjoy it and feel satisfied when I am done. I have no plans to increase the number of times a week I run or to run a marathon. I have reached this goal, and it fulfills my needs the way I had hoped.

It would have been easy for me to overreach by wanting to run five times a week or starting off by running three to five miles. This approach would have been too much to incorporate into my life. I would have set myself up for failure. Making lasting change in your life is about setting yourself up for success. This is what small, achievable goals do for you.

It's not just people who overreach. Businesses are also susceptible to setting themselves up for failure. More often than not, when an organization sets out to make change, it is done with large proclamations on a grand scale. And while this may have an initial surge of energy, it can also fizzle fast if there are no small wins. Very rarely can an organization make seismic shifts quickly or accurately with success. It is usually a cumulative effect of many small, thoughtful changes. People really do not readily embrace change. I have been witness to many corporate initiatives that have not lived to fruition, and it's usually because they were too cumbersome for people to incorporate into their already overburdened workloads. People can make small changes, and that is where you will find your success.

Put a Stake in the Ground

Halfway through my horrible year, I decided it was time to change the shape of my arc. I felt as though I needed to make a personal statement to proclaim that I was not going to let the events of that year get the best of me. At the time, I was still working in advertising and overseeing three accounts. Many of my colleagues were aware of the year that I was having and were very sympathetic. They all pitched in to help carry some of the business burdens. While talking to one of my colleagues, I realized it was time to celebrate all that is good, starting with my team. They worked hard and were very supportive of each other and me. We coined this the "It can't get any worse party." We took the afternoon off. We enjoyed food, drink, and games. It was important to me to make it fun and also reward those who were very generous with their support. I would not have been able to handle all that was put in front of me without a strong team. The gesture was modest but from the heart. In the end, it turned out to be very cathartic for everyone.

Sometimes, staring down your situation and changing the energy around it can be quite healthy. I wanted to send a signal that I wasn't going to roll over and be a victim of this situation or any situation. I had the power and fortitude to change the arc of my events. When you decide to reset your career and life, put a stake in the ground and proclaim that you are ready to take control.

Being Ruthless with Your Time

To be ruthless with your time means to cut out all that does not add value to your life. When I first started to incorporate this idea into my life, I struggled with how close it felt to being selfish. To really implement it, I had to reset my definition of *selfish*. Historically, I would accommodate the wants and needs of others before my own. This was across all aspects of my life. I was more apt to spend my time helping others than advancing my own success. I felt it would be selfish of me not to. The internal strife began to mount when I had to reconcile pursuing my newly articulated vision with how I had been in the past. There is not enough time in the day for me to pursue both full throttle. After some contemplation, I understood that placing more emphasis on living my vision is not selfish. It is being true to who I am and the impact I want to have. This meant I could no longer drop everything to assist others or feel compelled to do so. I had to get comfortable saying no as well as managing my instincts to want to help. In this case, saying no is not shutting out possibilities but rather making room for the possibilities that further my goals.

In the beginning, I had to really make a conscious effort to be ruthless with my time. I started doing it in small increments. First, I had to be clear about what I wanted to accomplish each day, each week, and each month. I was very specific in determining which situations I could say no to that would have little impact on my relationships or my work. What I found is that the overall quality of everything I did increased. I was doing what really mattered most, not only to me, but also to those closest to me. I also learned to be polite about saying no, especially to people to whom I had always said yes. During the first few years of starting my business, I had to put a sizeable amount of energy into getting it off the ground. This meant I was not always available for dinners or hanging out on weekends. I let my friends know that this was a critical time, and while I would always be there for them, I had to be judicious in how I spent my time.

Why are people so afraid of doing what they want? What would happen if more people set goals and focused on moving toward them? Would there be more inspired creativity? Would there be more happy people?

I Want a Balanced Life!!!

Before I close this chapter, I want to tackle this topic. Undoubtedly, one of your goals is to have a balanced life. I encounter countless people who are striving to reach this elusive goal. The concept of having a balanced life permeates discussions of harried professionals. Books, articles, and blogs have been written about it. News and lifestyle shows have produced segments on it. Images and infographics have visualized it.

Inherent to achieving a balanced life means finding a constant state of equilibrium—everyday you get to leave the office at a reasonable hour, you can attend your kid's soccer game, and work doesn't impinge on your personal life. You have time for everything and everyone in equal measure. And yet, therein lies the conundrum. On a daily basis, forces beyond your control challenge your ability and wherewithal to attain this fleeting state of harmony. There will be times when you have to work late, tend to family and health issues, travel over a weekend, or join a conference call from home. Practically speaking, this is how life works and is therefore seemingly at odds with living a balanced life.

Frustrations mount and disappointments reign when you try to reconcile the theory of a balanced life with the reality of what you face on a daily basis. So I put the question to you, is a balanced life what you really want or realistic to achieve? Are we just pining for something that is unattainable?

I found that seeking a balanced life was compromising my happiness. Even as a solo practitioner, a balanced life is out of my grasp. There are weeks when I'm working late and getting up early. There are times when family issues dominate my life. There are times when health issues challenge my ability to be energetic and productive. Not to mention a one-year period when my life was completely out of balance. After examining my own life as well as coaching hundreds of people (I hear this from men and women alike), I've come to the conclusion that a balanced life is a misnomer. Therefore, I've taken a new perspective. What if we aspire to live an integrated life? At the heart of an integrated life we are clear about what's most important, and we ensure these things are present in our life whether it is on a daily, weekly, monthly, or yearly basis. From my perspective, an integrated life is more within our control and allows for the natural ebb and flow of life and work.

Madeline, a highly competent, self-aware woman in her early forties, works full time, as does her husband, and they have two kids under the age of ten. To further complicate the current situation, her husband is completing his graduate degree, and they are renovating their home. Needless to say, this doesn't have the makings of a balanced life. How could it? On any given day, Madeline is taunted and teased with situations, big and small, beyond her control (the need to stay late at the office to finish an assignment, a broken furnace that needs to be replaced, a child who is struggling with math, etc.) that challenge her ability to find and maintain balance. Gripped with anguish that she is unable to create balance in the face of these daily events, she turns her emotions inward, chastising her inability to find balance in order to be a good employee, mother, spouse, friend, sister, and daughter. She's not able to reconcile the onslaught of "balance your life" messages with the realities of the life she has and loves.

Madeline realized that her emotional connection to achieving a balanced life was misplaced and leaving her forlorn. Once she shifted her orientation toward integration, she immediately felt relaxed. She seized this new view on how to manage her life and responsibilities. Her focus is now on what matters most at any given point in time, while staying mindful of the bigger picture to ensure one area isn't being dominated at the exclusion of another. Her notable revelation was to forgive herself. She's not perfect; life happens. As long as she is mindful of what matters most, she can be productive at work and present and loving with her family and friends.

Exercise: To begin, identify what's most important to you. An ideal place to start is your Life Line Assessment. What have you rated high, and what have you rated low and want to improve upon? For example, if you want to enhance your personal growth by getting involved in a community organization, look at your schedule and assess when and how you can integrate community service in your life. It may mean being creative and flexible with your commitment based on your work and family schedule. Some weeks you will have more time to dedicate than others. The same is true for attending your child's school activities, having dinner with your family, visiting your parents, reading a book, etc.

KEY QUESTIONS

· Are you making a pledge to thrive or to simply survive?

· What do you want to amplify in your life?

· How are you creating an action plan for your future? What are your Dynamic Goals?

· What are you doing to create space in your life to achieve your goals?

— CHAPTER FIVE —

A REASON TO BELIEVE

It is easier to embrace change and less daunting to go after your goals when you have something to believe in. What do you believe in? You may point to the doctrines of your religion. You may ponder the virtues of family and home. You may even reference the founding hallmarks of your government. But what do you really stand for? If you're speechless, you are like most people who have yet to form their own core belief system—a belief system that reflects how you want to live your life. Without one, you may not be living your life to the fullest and with conviction.

Now you may be wondering, what is a core belief system? Each of you, even those who claim to have little self-awareness, has some idea of what you believe in, what you want for your life, and the impact you want to have on others. These three elements are what make up your core beliefs. Articulating your core belief system is the next step, and it can be both rewarding and unsettling. Why unsettling? Because it requires ample amounts of thought and introspection. Furthermore, it may reveal that you have been living a life based on someone else's vision: maybe your parents', maybe your spouse's, or maybe what you thought you should be doing. Not to worry. Why you are where you are is not important. What matters now is that you are doing something to start living with clear intent. The reward of a core belief system is that you can start today to design the life you want, a life that will propel you forward and guide you no matter what situation you encounter.

Create Your Own Core Belief System

Where to begin? Focus on the here and now. You can easily get distracted trying to analyze why you have not done this yet, but that is futile and will only cloud your ability to move forward. I contend that most people are not ready to take on this endeavor until they have reached a level of life experience that will allow them to develop a core belief system that is thoughtful and rich.

Your core belief system consists of vision, values, and purpose. The three of these working together are powerful.

1. Your vision is an articulation of the career and life you want.
2. Your values are the core tenets of how you want to live your life.
3. Your purpose is the impact you want to have on others.

I will tell you now that you will challenge your intent throughout the entire process of outlining your core belief system. You will question whether you are developing the "right" system. You will question whether this is all a waste of time since nothing will change. You may think, "I could not possibly do what I want and change the direction of my arc." You are, after all, human. Always present will be the need to protect yourself from failure and disappointment. For most, that is what they know. Others, who have allowed themselves to believe in the idea of moving upward and accelerating, have redirected their lives with positive impact on the people around them.

The steps to developing a core belief system require time and a desire for change. It will take some positive energy; therefore, it is best to do it when you are feeling good. This could be at certain times of the day— after a workout, when you finish an assignment at work, or after a movie that has left you inspired. You will want to be at your best, with a clear mind. When I am working with clients who are feeling particularly down, I will avoid conversations about vision, values, and purpose. Their ability to focus is impaired and they typically prefer to talk out their current situation. When they are ready, we come back to their core belief system.

Now, there is a difference between putting a challenge like this aside for a day and completely pushing it to the back burner. Just because it is taxing does not mean it can be avoided. I have yet to meet a client who has not found value in going through the process. Rather, it makes people feel better since they have a clearer view of themselves. It becomes a valuable touchstone to keep them grounded, especially for those who are most susceptible to the whims of others. I take this seriously, both for my clients and for myself; however, it should also be fun and uplifting.

When you are ready, surround yourself with inspiration, whether that means listening to your favorite music, sitting in a comfortable chair, lighting a fire, relaxing outside with your morning coffee, or any other environment that helps you focus. Creating the mood will elevate your spirits and allow generous thoughts to flow freely. You can also ponder these questions while doing activities that are calming but also put you in motion, such as running, fishing, swimming, walking.

A core belief system will not only ground you but will elevate you. It will redirect your arc upward. This is about getting absolute clarity around what you want and making the commitment to live it. The end result is a core belief system that is so vibrant and true you feel it deep in your soul. It resonates to such an extent that you are motivated each day to live it and share it with others. During tough times, it can be your anchor. Without it you can be drifting aimlessly. Or worse yet, just surviving.

Julia's Story

Julia was a senior director for a small company where she worked for fourteen years. She was responsible for a staff of fifteen full-time and ten part-time employees. She was hardworking and unassuming. During her tenure with the company, she retooled the internal customer service department. Her responsibilities grew extensively, as reflected by the size of her team. She had very little formal leadership training and was relying on her experience, her knowledge of the business, and what she had learned from previous bosses and mentors. Basically, her learning was on the job. Due to the hectic nature of her management role, she had little time to reflect on her career, her leadership approach, and her future. However, when changes within her company began to occur, she realized the need to take a step back and develop a core belief system that would guide her throughout her career and life. ∽

In the next few pages we'll see how Julia used her core belief system to address work-related issues and create a path for the future.

The Relevance of a Vision

Let's begin by articulating your vision. This means tackling one big question: How do you want to be living your life? While this is big and broad, it can be broken down into a few focused areas: What do I enjoy doing, what do I stand for, what environment motivates me, and where do I see myself in the future?

For me, it started with my career. As I rose through the corporate ranks, it became increasingly clear how I wanted to conduct myself in business. I wanted to behave a certain way and be more selective in the types of people I do business with. In many respects, I wanted more impact, control, and creativity. The by-product of this would be fewer constraints and more freedom. This meant I had to get very clear about what I wanted to do. I had to do an incredible amount of soul-searching about what I truly wanted to do and what would make me fulfilled (versus what I thought I should be doing). This was a big shift for me. I had spent most of my adult life doing what I thought I should be doing. Once I freed myself from the shackles of the "right" thing to do, I was able to finally explore what I wanted to do.

Your vision needs to be steeped in something concrete and actionable. For you, it may mean creating systems and procedures that enable collaboration, or helping companies create sustainable business practices, or working for a company that is community- and family-oriented. For me, it meant exploring a way of life where I would have a personal impact on people. I knew I wanted the next phase of my life to be more meaningful and to give something back to humanity. Through my recent journey, I have realized there are many people in their forties who are struggling to find their way forward. At an age where they have the most to give and should be thriving, they are sliding into survival mode. Many have lost sight of who they are and what they want. Unfortunately, this means they are slowly giving away themselves to others until they no longer recognize who they are. In time, they become angry, frustrated, and disengaged. This insight became the underpinnings of my vision.

Once I figured out how to articulate my vision around what I wanted to do, there was no going back. In short order, I began to redesign my life. With each passing day, the vision for my life was slowly unfolding. And then one day, I experienced my period of illumination, when I could finally see the vision of my life. This had a profound impact on me and set in motion a new way of being. While it did not provide a detailed road map for how to achieve my vision, I had clarity about where to start and all the possibilities it entailed. And for once in my life, I had no doubt about what I was doing or how I would make it work. There is one thing I do know: My happiness comes from being true to myself.

Clients I work with really struggle to articulate a vision for themselves. Whenever I broach this topic, I can see them become visibly uncomfortable. They will fidget in their chair, avoid eye contact, and attempt to redirect the conversation. As soon as this starts, I steel myself because I am not going to let them squirm their way out of committing to a vision. Once I have their feet to the fire, the conversation usually starts with my favorite excuse: "Okay, let's do this, but I'm not in a position to make any substantive changes to my life." They become defensive and stand firm on why they can't make any change. The crack-up for me is that all I am asking people to do is to articulate their vision. There is no expectation that they will rush out, quit their job, and open a bike shop. I keep emphasizing that this is just an exercise, a place to start. It is the one time when you can suspend reality and focus on yourself. This usually takes a fair amount of coaxing to get started. In the beginning, people find it easier to talk in terms of pros and cons about their current job. This is all well and good, but it is too tactical at this point. I push them to focus on the bigger picture. There is a time and place for pros and cons, just not now.

Julia's Story

Julia, for the most part, was left to run her department and team autonomously. Never one to self-promote, she assumed her work spoke for itself and when senior management was ready, she would be promoted. Her philosophy was "If I take care of my people, I will be taken care of." This is an admirable approach and in theory a great practice. It works if your senior management subscribes to the same philosophy. In Julia's case, they had a different approach. On a cold, rainy afternoon she was informed that a new layer of management was being brought in between her and her current boss, who was a member of the senior team. Julia was devastated. How could this happen? The new boss was not only one of her peers but also a micromanager. That meant Julia had lost her autonomy, something near and dear to her, and it meant her career progression had stalled. She stuck it out for a while, being the good soldier, but after some time she realized that this was not a sustainable situation. ⤜

When she came to me, Julia was seeking advice on what to do. True to form, she came to the conversation with a list of pros and cons. I told her to put it aside and let us just talk about what she wanted to do. I asked her to think about this within the context of her current company as well as an ideal job with another company. About midway into the conversation, we hit what her ideal job would be. She got tremendous satisfaction creating, staffing, and leading internal customer operations. She was naturally wired to solve operation problems and had a knack for hiring and grooming people to be high performers. She also liked playing the role of the underdog and achieving success where others couldn't. I could already feel her energy level begin to rise as she described in great detail her ideal job.

We then discussed her current company. If she could have any role, what would it be? Surprisingly, she turned her attention to a position outside of internal customer service operations, and to a more external-facing role. While this was enticing, it was also accompanied by apprehension. "I am not qualified for that position," she said. I had to stop her. "Remember, we are just talking. This is not the time to shut down an idea." The more we talked about this option, the more she began to come up with ideas on how she could test the waters internally to see if this was even a viable option for her. That was a huge step forward. She could see a vision for herself that focused on creating, staffing, and leading a team that is either internal or external facing. This created multiple possibilities and a framework to have a conversation with her boss and the company's senior management about her future and what type of role excites her. She felt liberated knowing she was taking back control of her career.

Visions take time to implement and require a lot of patience. It took Julia two years to fully actualize her vision. In the beginning, she was collecting information by investigating, doing, asking, and listening. Having a vision was a new concept for her. In the past, she had lived her life around three objectives: to be financially secure, to be respected in her profession, and to spend time with friends and family. Now that she knows what she is working toward, she is fully engaged in living her vision.

How to Craft Your Vision

As you begin to formulate your own vision, take a moment now to write down your initial reactions to the following questions:

WHAT I KNOW ABOUT ME TODAY

- What are three things I like to do every day?
- What are the ten things I most enjoy doing?
- What makes me happy?
- What do I respond to?
- What type of environment stimulates and motivates me?
- What do I stand for?

WHAT I WANT FOR MY FUTURE

- Where do I want to be in five years and with whom?
- How do I want to live my life?
- If I never had to work another day in my life, what would I do?
- What is the theme for my life?

Get creative. You can articulate your vision using whatever means will help bring it to life: words, a vision board, music, analogies, metaphors, quotes, colors. It is your vision, and you need to be inspired by its expression.

Your vision is an articulation of the career and life you want.

The Value of Values

Most people have a vague sense of their values. I am reminded with each new client just how challenging a values discussion can be. Most people really struggle to name, let alone explain, their values. Some even get frustrated. And yet, a robust set of values serves as a vital filter to making decisions across all aspects of our lives. If one of your core values is adventure, and you do not honor and live to that value in some manner, you will constantly have a sense that something is missing in your life. This could result in feeling unfulfilled and unsatisfied. Think about what would change if you recognized and set out to honor that value. It may mean the difference between a run-of-the-mill vacation and one that challenges you to do something new and different. Think about how much more excited you would feel to plan something and how great it would be once you were there.

It is helpful to share your values with those people who are important in your life. If your family knows that adventure is important to you, it may bring out a sense of adventure in them. They may be more open to hiking down into the Grand Canyon instead of just viewing it from up top. Not only are you nurturing your own values, you are exposing them to new experiences. Conversely, some values are there for your own benefit. If one of your values is integrity, then you will always conduct yourself appropriately. You will also be keenly aware of others who exhibit the same trait. It may mean you shy away from those in whom it is not present.

Your values become an indispensable guide for making decisions. This is especially true when making big decisions such as a career change. Your values can be a touchstone for evaluating a new position or company. When you are interviewing, you can use your values as a guide. Does the company and its employees share your values? Is this a place where you can exercise your values? Your values also open up a whole new line of questions you may want to ask a potential employer. Your observations and decisions will be much more insightful. There may be times when you decide not to honor your values, but at least you enter into the situation with your eyes wide open and do not leave yourself susceptible to frustration. You will be able to better manage potentially challenging situations. Think about how much more fulfilled you will be the more you live your values.

Julia's Story

Julia had a natural ease with people and was able to motivate her team into action. She fostered a family-like atmosphere where people were very cordial to each other and typically worked well together. She was well liked by her team and was learning how to lead by setting expectations and having the team come together and actively develop a game plan for how to achieve the vision. This was new territory for Julia. In the past, she would be more direct in the "how" of achieving the vision. To her delight, the team embraced this challenge to develop a plan.

Julia sensed one member of the team was withdrawing from the others. He seemed preoccupied and tense. This change in behavior was also noticed by Julia's boss and another senior director. It became the topic of sidebar conversations between Julia and the other senior leaders. Speculation and assumptions were starting to be made. Julia was really struggling with how to manage this situation. The other senior directors were offering all kinds of advice based on their assumptions of what was going on. After a few weeks, Julia was at a crossroads. She knew this could not go on any longer, but she was struggling with how to broach the topic with her direct report.

While looking at her list of values posted in her home office, she realized what needed to be done. Her values are there to help guide her when making decisions and taking action. One of her values was openness. What if she approached the conversation through the lens of openness? This meant she would be open about what she was noticing and would be open to hear the response. While others around her were already speculating and hypothesizing (assuming the worst, as we are prone to do), she decided to approach the conversation with a clean slate.

That week she sat down with her direct report and talked about what she was noticing and the impact it was having. Before she could even finish, her direct report breathed a huge sigh of relief and began to speak. He had been contemplating going back to school for an advanced degree. This would not change his current position within the company, but it would entail him juggling classes and homework while still working a full-time job. He did not know how to have the conversation because he did not want to jeopardize his position. Julia was relieved. For weeks, this had been built up into something more than it was. Plus, she loved the fact that her direct report wanted to continue to further his professional development. She believed there was always a place for additional skills. Julia realized the importance of her values not only in how she wants to live her life but also in how she can use them to guide her through tough situations. ✍

Since your values are germane to you, when you use them to make decisions or approach tough situations it feels very genuine. It is hard to go wrong when you are being genuine and true to yourself. It will make you feel more comfortable and relaxed during a tough situation. You may not always have the outcome you desire, but those disappointments are often easier to accept when you know you have been true to yourself.

How to Craft Your Values

Here are five easy steps to help you articulate your values.

1. Grab a piece of paper and start generating a list without censoring or second-guessing.

Identifying values is not easy. I have many clients ask to choose from an existing list of values. I deny them the list. I believe each person needs to tap into their own creative being in order to discover what is important to him or her. If you pick from a list, then you will be more susceptible to choosing what you think are the "right" values. There is no right or wrong set of values.

2. Group like values together.

Your list may include ten, fifteen, or twenty values. I hope that it does. As you review your list, you will begin to notice similarities. Openness, honesty, and transparency may feel similar to you. Group like values together. Within each group, circle the value that best reflects you.

3. Pick your top five.

Once you have grouped similar values, your list is probably down to ten or fewer. This is when you have to start making some hard choices. What are your core values? What are the values that you hold near and dear to your heart? Go with your gut; do not second-guess yourself. This is not the time to think with your head. There will be plenty of exercises where you will use your head and logic, especially when you start planning for action. This exercise is all about your heart and what feels right.

4. Ensure your values cover many aspects of your life.

Take another look at the top five and ensure they are not just about your career or your family. Your values should represent the entire you. Many people who are very career focused will end up with values that represent them as professionals. While our careers may play a significant role in our lives, career shouldn't dominate the list. Some of your values will cross over from professional to personal, while others will have the most significance in your personal life.

5. Write a fifty-word paragraph on what each value means to you.

It is essential to not stop with just the list. What I have found is that people attach their own meaning to values beyond the standard word definition. If you value humor, you will want to understand what humor means to you. As you can imagine, humor comes in many shapes and sizes. There is sophomoric humor, sardonic humor, witty humor, silly humor. Be specific about what kind of humor you value. When you are finished, read the paragraph and circle the words that resonate the most. Select the one word that best describes that value. Understanding what your values mean to you will make them more personal and help you find the description that is just right for you.

You want your values to feel real and tangible. This is only for you, so it does not matter what you have written. Have fun and do not erase. Erasers are forbidden in this exercise. The more you capture your stream of thought, the more likely you will find hidden gems of meaning that capture the true essence of your values.

TIPS IF YOU ARE STUCK

· Think back on a time when you achieved success. What were you doing and how were you doing it?
· What drives you crazy? What is the opposite?

· What is nonnegotiable in your life?
· What do you obsess over?

By now, you have had a chance to craft your values. At least, I hope you have! I know I was one of those people who would read various self-help books, glance over the exercises, and then quickly turn the page, thinking that I would do them later. Well, later would never come, and I would finish the book feeling a bit inspired but with no action taken. It was not until I was going through the process of becoming a certified coach that I completed the values exercise. It was required, and I was being held accountable. When all was said and done, I fully realized the power of having a set of values that became the tenets by which I live my life. Everything became a bit easier, and I became more confident in my decision making. With that, if you haven't crafted your values, do so now, before moving on.

Your values are the core tenets of how you want to live your life.

The Pertinence of a Purpose

During the twenty-one years I spent in advertising, I was constantly on the hook to develop a purpose for my clients' brands. My team and I would spend hours, weeks, and sometimes months living our clients' brands in order to really get to know them. In some cases, "war rooms" were created so we could surround ourselves with the brand. We had research, competitive analysis, and brand history from which to draw. In most cases, a brand's purpose and values take on human-like traits. A commonly asked question we'd have to answer is "If this brand were a person, who would it be?" Having a finely tuned brand purpose was central to developing a new advertising campaign, new product development, and marketing communications. We were skilled at it and took great pride in the end product.

I have found it quite interesting to now work with advertising and marketing professionals as an executive coach. When the conversation turns to creating their purpose, the discussion comes to a screeching halt. Inevitably, their head tilts to the left (or right), and I can see their stumped look. It is as if they never thought about their own purpose. Within minutes, I will be asked, "Well, how do I do that?" And without missing a beat, I lean forward and say, "You have been doing this for your clients' brands for years and you have never thought about it for yourself." Well, truth be told, I never thought about my purpose either until it was part of a coaching exercise. But now, it is integral to who I am and how I want to be. My purpose is what propels me out of bed every morning. When I enter into a new situation, I ask myself, "Will this allow me to fulfill my purpose?" And at the end of the day, I can ask myself, "How much did I live my purpose?"

Defining your purpose has become central to many self-help books and philosophies. With that importance has come an enormous pressure to define your perfect purpose. People think it should be noble and carry a certain level of gravitas. Their purpose should be so outstanding that when they are at a cocktail party they will be proud to share their purpose and people will respond in awe. Herein lies the typical dilemma. "How will I know I have the 'right' purpose? I want mine to be impressive." This is when I have to stop the conversation and reset expectations. Your purpose is first and foremost for you. There is not a right or wrong purpose. One is not nobler than the next. Furthermore, the exact words you choose are not as important as the meaning. Does the meaning resonate with you? That is the essential question.

When I was going through the coaching certification process, we each had to come up with a purpose. We answered a series of questions and worked through our final articulation with the help of our fellow coaching cohorts using a defined structure. We then had to stand up and proclaim our purpose to the rest of the group. While mine was true to who I am, it was a bit clunky and over-the-top; but it was mine and I owned it. The underlying meaning brings a smile to my face and is reflective of me. As time passed, I continued to live my purpose. Then one day, I had an epiphany. My purpose is really quite simple: *hope creator*. When I am creating or enabling hope, I am at my best. Being a hope creator is about having an impact on others. The level of impact varies, but the intent is always the same. It is energizing and meaningful, and it keeps me grounded. Whenever I begin to question what I am doing and why I am doing it, I come back to my purpose. If I am creating hope, then I am living the best possible life for myself and for others around me. So while this book provides a structured approach to defining your purpose, it can also show up out of the blue.

Julia's Story

With a vision and set of values, Julia was making progress in crafting her core belief system. Despite her momentary setback with her new reporting structure, she felt she had achieved a level of success with her career. She was well regarded by her team and had a happy, well-adjusted family. The problem she faced now was she wasn't clear about the impact she wanted to have. She was very thoughtful and was looking for more meaning in her life moving forward. The accumulation of material possessions was ringing hollow. While Julia was defining her values, she was becoming aware of a common theme, local influence. She was intrigued by the idea of giving to others and sharing her knowledge and expertise in a way that would help people make better, more-informed decisions. This led Julia to realize her purpose is about making others successful by sharing best practices that would help other local businesses succeed. She spent time articulating what that means to her and how she can put it into action. Turns out, she was already putting this into practice with the advice and counsel she was providing to a neighbor who owns a technology software company. But now she could leverage it to a greater extent. This meant jumping on relevant opportunities at her job to be more external facing and redefining her role within her company to include community outreach. It allowed her to bring new ideas to her company that were well received. One reason for this is that her ideas came from a very authentic place, and Julia could really get behind them. It was easy for her to talk about them, and her enthusiasm became infectious. Others wanted to be part of what she was doing. And most important, Julia now has a clear understanding of what keeps her motivated. ⤸

Your purpose is central to who you are in all aspects of your life. Having a purpose means living your life with intent each and every day. It permeates everything you do, how you are being, and your interactions with others. Your purpose represents your true essence as a human being. It's the heart of who you are.

How to Craft Your Purpose

Answer these questions to help you discover your purpose.

LOOK INWARD

- When I am at my best, I am . . .
- When I am most alive, I am . . .
- When I am most present and engaged, I am . . .
- What are my special, unique skills?

LOOK OUTWARD

- What is the greatest impact I have on others?
- What do others respond to when I am around?
- When do others lean on me?

INTANGIBLES

- How do people typically describe me?
- What do I want to be known for?

The idea of a purpose for some seems very lofty, like monumental missions such as world peace or fighting poverty. "Why do I need one?" they wonder. I firmly believe that all of us have contributions to make. The clearer we are on what those are, the better chance we have to act on them, and the more fulfilled we'll be.

Your purpose is the impact you want to have on others.

You and Your Core Belief System

The best part of your core belief system is that it is yours and yours only. It is not to be judged, evaluated, or critiqued by anyone else. Committing your core belief system to paper is not the same as etching it in stone.

Your core belief system is living, breathing, and evolving just like you. It can be neat and tidy or sloppy and messy. The important thing is to start living it, now. Do you feel more empowered now that you know what your core belief system is? Is it bringing some clarity to how you think and relate to other people? Does it paint a clear picture of who you are? Does it put into words what you have been feeling and thinking all along? If these beliefs are true to you, there should be an element of "Yeah, that is exactly me, but I have never been able to put it into words." Most people find comfort in finally being able to see it written on one page. A common response is "Why haven't I done this before?" Not to worry. It is not an easy thing to articulate. Most people want to judge themselves or, better yet, have someone else evaluate what they have done for validation. Guess what? For once, the only validation you need is your own. No one is better suited to knowing whether your core belief system is true to yourself than you. Neither is it graded nor does it get passed up the chain of command for approval.

As you begin to put your core belief system into practice, you will find you are less likely to be spinning your wheels or feeling guilty about doing some things and not others. One of my core values is being physically fit. Every day I am confronted with how I should be spending my time, especially when I initially started my coaching practice. Not only did I have a pretty full coaching schedule but I was also writing a weekly blog, working on this book, and still making time for friends and family. On many occasions, as I was headed out to the gym, I would question whether or not I should be taking an hour and a half out of my day to go work out. The answer was always a resounding yes. If I am going to live my values, then I have to be true to them. I knew that if I did not go to the gym then I wouldn't feel my best. This helped me make decisions about other activities that did not fit my core values. A core belief system is especially helpful for people who tend to be swayed by others. When you have something to anchor yourself, you are less likely to lose your way.

KEY QUESTIONS

· What is your core belief system?
· How does your core belief system amplify your life?

STEP THREE

CONQUERING OLD FOES

CHAPTER SIX

WHAT DOES SUCCESS LOOK LIKE?

In chapter 3, I introduced the Seven W.A.R.N.I.N.G. Signs of Distress and how to spot them in your own life. Through the experiences of Simon (wavering self-confidence), Ethan (at sea), Miguel (relinquished identity), Marina (neglected), Danielle (idling), Anna (no focus), and Patrick (growing discontent) you also saw the impact these warning signs can have on all facets of a person's life. Each of these people witnessed his or her life arc quickly descending but had no idea what to do about it.

Well, I have good news to report. With some hard work and commitment, they were able to change the arc of their life and head in a new direction. Let's see how they did it.

Simon Has Restored His Confidence

Simon was beginning to feel old before his time. As a shy person, he found it was getting harder to have his voice heard. He wanted to be more open and express himself through his thoughts and ideas. It was time for Simon to see himself as he really was. No longer was he discounting the value he could bring to others. He embraced his smarts and his creativity. He also acknowledged that he was best in a team, particularly a team of like-minded individuals who want to create new ways of working. He realized and accepted that he had no visions of being in management or the lead of a team. His contributions were most applicable within the team itself. Helping to bring everyone else along in a way that brings harmony and forward movement was his greatest contribution. This was very enlightening for Simon. Historically, he believed, as conventional wisdom would say, that the only path is upward to management and the corner office. He was delighted to uncover his role as the "glue" to be far more fulfilling and rewarding than being at the top of an organizational chart. He relished the camaraderie of the team and working side by side with his peers.

While Simon would never admit this, he found his leadership role; it is just defined differently from the textbook definition. He had rediscovered happiness and contentment from his work, his creative hobbies, and his family and friends. I would presume they have also encountered a much more engaged, vibrant, and animated person.

Simon's core belief system

Vision: "Be real" and live life in a genuine way

Values: Atmosphere of creativity, genuineness, being relaxed, commitment, gratitude

Purpose: To be the glue that holds people and projects together

Ethan Is No Longer at Sea

For Ethan, redirecting his life was about letting go of the baggage associated with what was happening with his current job and the changes that were taking place. Realizing he could not control management and personnel changes, Ethan had to get clear about his career goals and aspirations. This was the first time since college that he felt he was not clear about what he wanted to do with his career. He had become so swept up in living the corporate mission that he forgot to check in with himself.

As his life was changing both at the office and at home, he needed to reinvent himself. His situation was no longer self-sustaining. More important, he was ready to reactivate his career. This meant an honest assessment of his skills and what type of work excited him. He was high energy and relished being in a dynamic work environment. Ethan was able to articulate that he most enjoyed the opportunity for responsibility and being the center of action. Once he came to terms with the fact that it was time to move on from his current employer, he was able to investigate other opportunities that would more closely align with his core belief system. In the end, it meant leaving his job and joining a new company and a new industry.

Ethan's core belief system

Vision: I want to live my life as a participant

Values: Energy, character, loyalty, learning, light-hearted humor

Purpose: I exist to help people grow and better themselves

Miguel Has Regained His Identity

It was important for Miguel to be his own person. He had to move away from the notion of having people like him at all cost. He found the courage to start living his life based on his vision. This was not being selfish, but rather, being empowered. First of all, Miguel accepted that he belonged in the position he had attained at the company he felt lucky to have joined twenty-one years earlier. This meant shedding the notion that others somehow knew more than he or were better equipped for a leadership role. He started trusting his instincts and consulting his values when making decisions. Miguel also adopted new behaviors that would lead to greater professional and personal success. Primarily this entailed not rescuing everyone else in order to make up for their shortfalls. He delegated responsibilities according to others' abilities and relied on them to hit their deadlines without him hovering to help. Additionally, he sought to find balance between work and home. His kids were at an age where being present for certain activities was important. This meant leaving the office between 5:00 and 5:30 p.m. to see them. Finally, Miguel wanted to get in better shape. He found it hard to make the time, as he was constantly connected to the office either by email or his phone. After much cajoling, he agreed to start running in the morning instead of reading his email. This was met with much trepidation, but once he came to terms with the fact that nothing earth shattering was happening at 6:00 a.m., he was able to make a morning run part of his regular routine.

Miguel's journey toward a great personal identity will be an ongoing process, but he was actively putting in place a new way of being that aligns with his personal and professional goals.

Miguel's core belief system

Vision: Owning my life and not feeling encumbered by what others think

Values: Optimism, integrity, trustworthiness, freedom, playfulness

Purpose: Instill greater humanity and acceptance in the workplace

Marina Is Back in Control

Marina took a leap and found a position at another small, closely held company. For Marina, the sense of family at work was paramount to her success and happiness. Her new boss was thrilled to have her on board and sought her involvement in key decisions. Marina had rediscovered her energy and enthusiasm for her job and her life. She feels valued and appreciates the stability and support of her new company.

Marina's core belief system

Vision: Live a rich, full life of learning and giving back

Values: Trust, learning, dependability, selflessness, young at heart

Purpose: Elevate the well-being of others through intellectual stimulation (challenge)

Danielle Is No Longer Idling

It was important for Danielle to rekindle her creative passions of photography, writing, and painting. While these were always present in her life, they often took a backseat to meeting the needs of others. These hobbies required her to carve out periods of time for intense focus. This meant less time catering only to her family. Danielle was worried that her family had come to rely on her involvement in all aspects of their lives. In a sense, she was being held hostage to their wants and needs, admittedly by her own choice. She anticipated pushback and disappointment; however, surprisingly she was greeted with encouragement. This was a major release of pressure. Danielle loved the idea of immersing herself in her passions. These solitary pursuits provided her a great deal of satisfaction and pride, not to mention some alone time to rejuvenate her spirit.

From a career perspective, she realized that she wanted an assignment with more creativity, the ability to work independently, and a flexible schedule. She was able to articulate this to her employer and hold firm while figuring out her next move. She no longer felt hostage to her job but could see opportunities. In the end, she was able to work with her employer to find a solution to meet both their needs.

Danielle's core belief system

Vision: Gain fulfillment from creativity and being singularly engaged in those pursuits

Values: Playfulness, learning different perspectives, friend-ships, creativity, alone time

Purpose: To help people see a new way of putting things together using words, images, and color

Anna Has Her Focus Back

Setting boundaries had always been a challenge. It was important for Anna to really get clear about her vision and empower herself to say no to everything else. She had a lot of interests and was really good at many of them. But she realized she had finite time in each day and had to let go of some wants to ensure she had time for her family and exercising. Armed with her core belief system, Anna started engaging in conversations with her boss about her ideas for new programs that she could initiate. Her boss welcomed these ideas and was particularly inspired by Anna's passion. He supported her, and she eagerly began the process of taking these ideas from doodles on paper to fully executed ideas. This meant she had to gain consensus and buy-in from other key internal stakeholders as well as continue with the responsibilities of her current job. Although this increased her workload in the short term, she was eager to bring her ideas to fruition. Along the way, there were concessions and periods of frustration; however, she was so clear about her vision she was able to negotiate solutions that kept the project moving. The day it was fully realized was satisfying; she was doing what she wanted to do. A new chapter began.

Anna's core belief system

Vision: To be part of building something that has social value

Values: Variety, independence, excellence, action, creativity

Purpose: Move and transform people by expanding their minds

Patrick Feels Fulfilled

The key task for Patrick was to let go of things that were no longer of interest. He was very clear about what he wanted to do. Unfortunately, it was not what he was doing, and that created internal strife. He saw opportunities within his company that aligned with his interests. To pursue them meant taking a risk and giving up his current position—and the role of the expert along with it. While he was ready to move on and tackle this new challenge, his company was not on the same page. His knowledge and expertise were valuable to them in his current role, and they were moving very slowly to implement his wishes. He saw the impact of what he could do in this new position, and yet he felt held back. This created even more frustration.

Because Patrick had a strong track record with his company and solid relationships with key executives, he was able to openly discuss his career aspirations and the desire for change. In preparation for these discussions, it was imperative for Patrick to demonstrate how a change for him would be a positive change for the company. Anticipating that there would be resistance to abandoning his current position, he knew that having a succession plan would help ease the concerns. This rested on his shoulders, but it made entertaining this change palatable. The change did not happen overnight, but it did happen, and Patrick is happily ensconced in his new role.

Patrick's core belief system

Vision: To proactively manage my career to ensure
I am challenged and acquiring new knowledge and skills
Values: Discovery, being goofy, generosity, storytelling,
traditions
Purpose: Be more engaged with others

It is always tough for people to believe that they can actually change their environment and themselves. This is particularly true for conformists and people who play by the rules. They are almost too respectful of themselves and others. The belief is that if they do a good job, they will get noticed and will be rewarded. While on the surface this should be true, not everyone is using this playbook. So regardless of whom you are working for, you have to have a clear understanding that you can change yourself but not necessarily the environment. It is okay to have your own wants and desires. In my opinion, the closer those link to those of your company, the better it is for everyone. If your current situation is not working for you, you do not have to accept it as your fate. You can set forth a new vision.

Uncovering Universal Themes

Some common themes begin to emerge as people slow down and discover what's most important in their lives. These work hand in hand with one's core belief system to enhance their way of being. As you look at your own life, you will probably see these same themes appear. You may find it helpful to discover how these play out in others' lives as well and how you can implement them. We will look at each one in turn.

- Being Creative
- Being Valued
- Being Unburdened
- Being Thoughtful
- Being Yourself

Being Creative. People can be creative in a variety of ways. The key is for you to have a creative outlet that is not judged by others. You do it for yourself, first and foremost. This should be something that provides pure joy.

Over and over again, as people collect responsibilities, they engage in fewer creative endeavors. The time set aside for creative activities gets squeezed out by the ever-present to-do list. And yet creativity is one of the best ways to keep you fresh and engaged. It allows you to open your mind and experiment. Somewhere along the way, as we age we seem to lose our ability to experiment, wonder, and play. We become heavily reliant on just doing all the stuff. Even at work, the fun can easily get sucked out of projects.

Some of this is caused by stress. When we are feeling pressured, we are less likely to be creative and more likely to be pragmatic. This is especially true if we have overcommitted ourselves. These feelings are often caused by our sense of obligation. Parents seem most susceptible. In today's world, parents have an incredible sense of obligation to be fully engaged with their kids' school, sports, activities, friends, and more. Being so involved takes up an enormous amount of time. And it happens at the expense of their own hobbies and interests. I remember parents of my generation (including mine) being involved but by no means omnipresent. Both my parents had their hobbies and interests, and they made time for them.

Somewhere along the way, feeding our own creative curiosity became less important. And I blame us. We allowed it to happen. I am guilty of this as well. I was so focused on my career that I didn't make time for creative outlets. Honestly, I felt it was wasteful. I had become very pragmatic in how I spent my time, most of which was spent tending the to-do list or working. I consider this particularly shameful because I worked in a creative business, but I wasn't allowing it to come out in my personal life.

Shortly after I began coaching, I attended a large dinner party, and seated next to me was a woman in her mid- to late sixties. We started off the conversation with the usual pleasantries. Turns out she is an artist, a painter. People whose occupations are outside corporate America always fascinate me. As we are chatting away, I learn that she started painting after the age of fifty. Her previous career was in corporate America. I asked why she never painted before. She told me she did not think she was good at it based on the opinions of teachers from high school, and then she became too busy with career and family. Later in her life, she decided to give it a try and started taking some drawing and painting classes. Before she knew it, she realized she had a gift for painting. What I found even more striking was that she believes the absence of a good or nurturing teacher in high school kept her from pursuing it in earnest at a young age.

This was one of the early conversations I had in which I began to realize that you can redirect your life. Here is someone who completely changed her vocation and how she was using her brain. Her corporate job was very left-brain and structured. Her career as a painter is unstructured and very right-brain. Best of all, during the entire dinner conversation, she was excited and engaged about her life and what she is doing. This was so refreshing and inspiring. She did not let her past (way past) experience dictate what she did in the future.

When people do speak of creativity and what they used to do, you can see how their mood lightens and it ignites a spark. I believe that we all have flames of creativity. Creativity, as I am defining it, is engaging in any activity that is created in your imagination and executed by you. This can be the very act of having a vision and bringing it to life. This can be with a piece of wood, a piece of paper and pencil, or a can of spray paint. It is about letting go and having fun. I can't overemphasize the importance of feeding our inner creative beings.

In a TIME/MPAA/Microsoft survey, 91 percent of respondents said creativity is important in their life, 83 percent said it's important in their personal life, and 65 percent said creativity is central to America's role as a global leader.[2]

Being Valued. People want to feel respected and appreciated, whether it is on a small or large scale. We want recognition for our contribution. This is true for the help we provide our friends, the effort we put forth at work, and the sacrifices we make for our family. The other side of the coin is valuing others.

Something very strange happens as we spend more time in our careers. Often, we get less praise and encouragement. Yet, this is the time when we should be getting more. We have more responsibility, we have more stress, and we are probably less secure about what we are doing because the weight of our decisions carries more meaning and impacts more people. In truth, most people can manage their jobs fairly well without much praise and encouragement, but only to a point. Without some assurance that you are being appreciated, it can begin to subvert your psyche (questioning your value). Which in turn can cripple your health (working too much and not taking care of yourself). Which in turn can undermine your overall well-being (not spending enough time with your family or doing the things you enjoy).

I remember early in my career, a friend, who was also in advertising told me a story about his boss, a senior leader within the advertising agency. They had just finished a huge client presentation. This was an important presentation and his boss had an active role in the meeting. As they were exiting the client's office his boss asked him, "How did I do? Did I do okay?" My friend reassured him that he did a great job and the meeting was a success. This left my friend feeling both grateful that his boss thought highly enough of his opinion to ask but also a bit perplexed as to why someone at such a high level would be seeking reassurance from someone his junior. I remember us talking about it over a beer and finding it very strange. Is he that insecure? He has done this hundreds of times. What's the deal? We finished our beers and didn't think much of it. Then I began to experience a similar thing, senior folks fishing for compliments.

I continued to find this odd, until I became one of those senior guys. What I learned is that after a while, the "'at a boy" or "great job" or "you really knocked it out of the park" comments stop. They just stop. Is it the competitive nature of being at the top and knowing only a few can really survive long term? Is it that it is assumed you do not need it because you know what you are doing? Is it that we just forget to do it because we are too busy? I am not exactly sure why. But I do know that it is common and widespread. If you are not getting encouragement freely, you then have to pander for it. I have to admit, I would even find myself seeking a level of reassurance that I was still adding value.

While money, title, office, and perks are all extrinsic motivators, there is no substitute for intrinsic motivators such as being valued. When people know their work is appreciated, they are more likely to be more engaged and creative. They will feel good about themselves and the company. This will spread outward to others both within and outside of the organization when they speak highly of the company. Personal relationships follow a similar pattern. We are more likely to do for others who we know will appreciate our effort. It is pretty simple.

The unfortunate truth is that many people do not feel valued, especially at work. They are not sure if they are completely supported and if someone has their back. This makes them feel vulnerable and unsteady. Some corporate cultures may like that, as they believe this type of tension brings out the best in people. While this may be a short-term strategy, I have yet to see it work over the long term. The extrinsic motivators will only last so long because they are not satisfying us on all levels. Clearly, senior leaders who have all the extrinsic trappings of success are still craving someone to say, "You did a great job."

Valuing someone and their effort should never be taken for granted. People want to be recognized for their work at every level. Take the time to let someone know when they have done a great job and, more importantly, that the organization is better off with them on the team. I know for the jaded few out there that this sounds a bit soft and corny. However, I would ask you to think about what really motivates you. I am sure you will find deep in the recesses of your being that you also want to know that your contributions and your presence in the office are appreciated and valued.

According to a survey by the American Psychological Association (APA), feeling valued is a key indicator of job performance. Employees who feel valued are more likely to be engaged in their work and feel satisfied and motivated.[3]

Being Unburdened. Over the years, you become aware of all that is not right, and lose sight of all that is right. Finding lightness in your way of being does wonders for your effort to thrive. It is hard to move forward when you have two tons of burden weighing you down.

It is really easy and really common to pick up another's baggage as you progress through life. And you pick up baggage from multiple sources. At work, you pick up the stress of doing a good or great job. Early on, you are trying to learn the ropes and prove yourself. This is a frustrating time because you know nothing and there is a lot to learn. In order to survive and prove your worth, you may start taking on tasks that really belong to someone else. An example may be when you are working on an assignment and others are not pulling their weight. You feel a sense of responsibility and you do not want to make waves, so you start compensating for others who are not doing their job well. Now you are doing your job and part of theirs. Without keeping this in check, you could find this a part of how you operate and what others expect. Because you have taken on that burden in the past, you automatically begin to do it even before it is necessary. "It is okay, just give it to me." "I'll do it because I know it will get done right. Or at least according to my standards." Others notice and assume you will take a project to the finish line. As a result, they do only as much as they feel is required, knowing you will do the rest.

You take on burdens at work because you think it will make you invaluable and untouchable should there be a workforce reduction. Because you are fearful of something bad happening, you try to compensate for it. While that tactic may work for a time, it is not an insurance policy for guaranteed employment. Later into my career, I became aware of how many burdens from others I was carrying, not only within my own company but also with my clients. It wasn't unusual for me to pick up the slack in order to keep projects moving along instead of holding others accountable. I learned how to let go of being the knight in shining armor. Sometimes you have to allow for failure in order for people to step up.

You may also take on family burdens. In every family and every relationship there are those who compensate for others. This is often done to keep harmony. If there is discord in the family, you take action in order to calm the waters. To make your parents proud, you do more than is expected. Further down the road, you may be the one to care for your parents as they age, while other family members are not present and involved.

In relationships, if you want someone to love you, you will do anything to win his or her affection and let the person off the hook. "It is okay, I'll take care of the grocery shopping while you play golf." This is true for men and women. It is equal opportunity. Over time, however, this behavior can cause resentment and anger. And it is robbing you of precious time to do things (hopefully being creative) that bring you pleasure and joy. Instead, you are the one doing all the chores, and you feel the weight of having to fit it all in during the course of a day.

The double whammy is if you are taking on burdens at work and at home. For most, it can go unnoticed, but it becomes heightened when life begins to throw a series of curve balls at us. Let's say you are having health issues and are no longer able to do as much. And yet, everyone is so accustomed to your extra effort that they see this change as you not pulling your weight. You have created a standard of expectation. Over the years you may have taken on so much of others' stuff that you aren't even in touch with who you are and what you want. That is when you have to let go of the baggage.

We may also take on the burdens of the greater society in which we operate. Often this comes in the form of judging others and taking on the ill feelings that are associated with that. You become irate if the service at a restaurant is not to your liking. You become ill-tempered if there is a long wait at a store. You are suspicious of other people, thinking that everyone is out to get you. Consider how much anger is coursing through your veins when you approach the world this way. Nothing good comes of being angry and judgmental all the time. Proof is that when you do it, you feel worse, not better. If this is one of your struggles, listen, and I mean really listen, to what you say and how you say it. Better yet, record yourself. Then ask yourself if you would want to be around that person.

Taking on burdens may make you feel good and accepted in the beginning, but it can be debilitating later. These burdens take away our power—especially our power to see clearly. We allow burdens too much influence in our lives, especially when that influence is linked to fear. Holding on because of fear is not a long-term strategy.

When we take on the burdens of others, we squeeze out the activities and tasks that bring us joy. Determining what is most important and letting go of the rest is key.

Those who face that which is actually before them, unburdened by the past, undistracted by the future, these are they who live, who make the best use of their lives; these are those who have found the secret of contentment.

—ALBAN GOODIER

Being Thoughtful. The more comfortable you are moving toward what you want, the more thoughtful you will be during the process. If you are settled and clear, you can better relate to others and give of yourself.

Nothing can be more welcoming than a gesture of thoughtfulness. How many times have you been genuinely touched when someone does something that is very kind? When it's also unexpected, we give double bonus points for the effort. Being thoughtful doesn't have to be big and it doesn't have to cost anything. It can start with greeting everyone with a smile. A friendly smile is a very thoughtful gesture that puts people at ease and makes them feel good. In fact, I am smiling as I write this section. I am not a natural smiler, but I found people and even animals are much more receptive when I am smiling.

I also believe in the common courtesy of holding the door open for others. This is another simple, thoughtful gesture that most people appreciate. I've always been apt to hold a door for others or wait for women to exit an elevator before I do. This seems the polite, thoughtful thing to do. I remember that I used to get a little hot under the collar if my thoughtful gesture was not acknowledged. In fact, I would take on this as a burden. I might even make a snide comment such as "You're welcome." One day,

I stopped the snide comments because I realized that it was taking away from my thoughtfulness. Why let one or two bad apples spoil it for me when most people are appreciative and gracious? Now, not only do I hold the door, but I also smile.

Being thoughtful has the greatest impact when you do it without hesitation, lending a helping hand to someone who is struggling with packages, offering to help with a party by bringing your favorite dessert, or taking a friend to coffee when you know he or she needs a compassionate ear.

Thoughtfulness is also acknowledging others. It is extremely powerful to acknowledge those around us, what makes them special and the times when they have been particularly helpful. I conduct a coaching skills workshop, and this is one of the skills that we teach—how to give an acknowledgment that has impact. It is not uncommon to acknowledge the task someone has done or to say "thanks" for doing the status report, for example. This is warranted but not really thoughtful. It is easy and can be easily dismissed. We may also string a few comments together so that our compliment might not at all register with the person, or the person may be selective in what he or she hears, and it could be the thing of less importance. Finally, many people have a hard time finishing their thought succinctly. They will begin with a really nice acknowledgment and then keep talking, and the acknowledgment may devolve into more work and other tasks. When the conversation is done, the acknowledgment has been lost and so has the person's thoughtfulness.

Here are a few simple pointers. A thoughtful acknowledgment should focus on something that is core to the person's being. Keep it short and stop talking as soon as you say it. Making the acknowledgment about the person and not what tasks he or she does will make it resonate much deeper. Keeping it short means it does not get watered down with a bunch of other meaningless stuff. Shutting up after you have said it will ensure that it sticks.

You may wonder if this works. Months after conducting this workshop, I was speaking to one of the participants. She was pleased to let me know that this "acknowledgment thing," as she called it, really worked. She relayed the story of how she was working with a colleague from another department on a project. When the project ended, she paid her colleague an acknowledgment. Her colleague was beside herself. She was so touched that someone would be so kind and thoughtful. She went on to say that she would be more than happy to work on other projects with her or help out. In the end, both people felt great about themselves and each other. And how long did the act of thoughtfulness take? Probably not much more than thirty seconds.

Being thoughtful is not labor intensive and yet has great rewards.

I always prefer to believe the best of everyone. It saves so much trouble.
—Rudyard Kipling

Being Yourself. Reclaim who you are and what is most important. This means being able to articulate it to yourself and others. Not everyone wants to run a company, start their own business, or be a millionaire. But people do want to feel fulfilled, energized, and engaged with their life. How to achieve that is probably not crystal clear. To bring clarity takes a plan, discipline, and a desire to thrive. Ideally, you do not want to leave anything on the table.

A big part of being you is mourning the death of achievements that never will be. In order to make room for new, more resonant goals, you have to let go of those that will never come to pass. It is not just about letting them go, however; it is also about replacing them. There is a little strategy I use to help put what I have to mourn in context with what I want to do. I take a piece of paper and draw a line down the middle. On the left side I write "I will not . . ." and then on the right side I write "But I will . . ." Earlier in the book I mentioned that I had to let go of the notion that I would become an executive vice president or higher at the advertising agency where I worked. This was tough for me, as I saw that as part of my plan and how I would be judged versus others. The flip side of it was that by starting my own business, I would be my own boss. This was very powerful to me. I was able to let go because I knew what I was working toward. To effectively let go of something you have wanted in the past, it needs to be replaced with something meaningful for the future.

There was an unintended consequence to my doing this. It also freed me. I was not only holding on to the outcome, but I was also restrained in how I was being. It wasn't until I let go that I realized how much I had been sacrificing myself in order to go after the "right" thing. This was really causing internal strife, especially as I progressed through my career.

Being yourself, if you have not been doing it lately, is not an easy thing to step into. It does not feel immediately comfortable, and you may question if this is the real you, especially if it has been tucked away.

Being yourself means tapping into your creativity and allowing yourself to express what is inside you however you like. It means valuing others and seeking out situations where you will be valued. It means being unburdened of all the stuff that is really meaningless and holds no power in how we live our lives. It means taking the time to be thoughtful and acknowledging others. We all want to be seen, especially by people we care about.

Be yourself; everyone else is already taken.

—OSCAR WILDE

KEY QUESTIONS

· What are you doing to be creative?
· What do you value in yourself?
· What are you doing to unburden yourself?
· What are you doing to be thoughtful?
· What are you doing to be yourself?

A powerless being fights against what he or she doesn't like. A powerful being supports what he or she believes in.

CHAPTER SEVEN

TAKE BACK YOUR LIFE.
CONQUER OLD FOES.

There comes a time in your life when you realize that no matter how much you try, you cannot control all that happens. What you can do is focus your energy on what is most important and then live to your core belief system. To do this, you have to release the need to control everyone and everything. When you reach this stage, it is quite freeing and energizing. This is when you can truly thrive.

For many of us, letting go of control is easier said than done. Putting change into action can be daunting, and keeping the momentum going takes commitment. I would be doing you a disservice to say that living your core belief system and embracing change is going to be easy. That's because clarity of your core belief system requires you to untangle some competing internal voices that may be at odds with your desire to adopt a new way of being. I would also be doing you a disservice to not support you and encourage you to step outside your current situation and push your boundaries. Initially, the change will be reflected in how you feel and how you see the world. Any substantive and lasting change has to begin inside. With the work you have done so far, you have the ability to create a new way of being.

What do I mean by a new way of being? Let me explain with an anecdote. As part of the coaching certification process, I participated in individual supervision sessions. My first individual supervision was with a wonderful and wise coach, Judith Cohen. The purpose of the supervision is to have a master coach listen and to critique your coaching sessions. I remember being nervous the first time I submitted my recorded session. But Judith made me feel so comfortable, and we hit it off from the outset. Our supervision calls were one part evaluation and one part philosophical discussion about *being* and what that means. From the beginning, she prodded me to dive deep into this concept. While the topic was extremely interesting, I was not sure where to begin—not to mention the fact that I had a very focused agenda of completing my certification and figuring out where my own life was headed. As any good coach does, she kept after me. Her belief in me as a coach and as a person lifted me up and carried me through the entire certification process. I successfully completed my certification and launched my coaching practice, but I was still left with this question: What is *being*?

For me, *being* means bringing forward the best part of me. This entails getting clear about what those best bits are. My core belief system highlights those best bits, and when I am living according to those, I am being true to myself, starting from the inside. My coaching style has always been grounded in respect, openness, compassion, empathy, and a commitment to speaking the truth, which is reflective of me. I listen, look beyond the obvious, and help clients uncover their truths. This has served me well as I work with clients to help them figure out how to integrate their core belief system into their life and their career.

There is one aspect of my coaching that is less practical and pragmatic, however. I have no scientific data to validate this theory; I just believe it to be true. I believe when you are clear about your core belief system and make it your way of being, change begins to occur. The very act of putting it out there will make it visible for the universe to see and understand. The more the universe can understand what you want and your way of being, the more likely it will send you or make available to you what you need. I admit, this may seem a bit out there and I have no academic evidence to back it up. But I do have my clients and myself as case studies. People begin to notice and experience change. They see opportunities that they might not have before. The result is greater awareness of their being. If you are willing to take this leap, you will find out what can be.

Your Saboteurs (Friend or Foe)

By now, you have made a commitment to thrive and change the arc of your life. You have diligently completed your core belief system and crafted your Dynamic Goals. But there are some niggling little voices in the back of your head that are taunting you, questioning you, and challenging your desire to disrupt the status quo. These inner voices have also been called saboteurs, gremlins, and blind spots. For the purpose of this book, I will refer to them as saboteurs because one of my clients liked the word so much. "I call them what they are: nasty, pain-in-the-ass little buggers that keep me from doing what I want."

First of all, it is important to embrace these voices. You will not vanquish your saboteurs; they are yours and will always be there. The point is to quiet them. They should be nothing more than a whisper. They do have a role and that role is to keep you in check. But it should be just that—a check.

Saboteurs are sneaky. They have the uncanny ability to say whatever will keep us in our comfort zone, and they creep up right when we are getting ready to make a change. Often, they are trying to protect us from spectacular failure, but they also keep us from spectacular success. For most people our internal voices have been a steady companion since we were young kids. They can either be germane to who we are (nature) or come from the environment in which we grew up (nurture). These inner voices not only reside inside our head but also manifest physically. This can be in the form of sweaty palms, a pit in your stomach, or heavy breathing. This double dose of fear can be debilitating. You may say to yourself, "I am physically feeling it and my brain is telling me to be cautious." That is really tough to ignore.

But do not despair; you can effectively quiet your saboteurs. First, you need to identify them. This requires you to get really conscious about what is happening in your life. Ask yourself, what do you shy away from because you might fail? When do you question yourself and your abilities? Where are you living small? Living small means not granting the world access to all that you have to offer. This, to me, is the most disheartening misdeed of the saboteurs. They deprive the world of thriving people.

To uncover even more saboteurs, look for patterns in your behavior. Some of the most common are creating distance from others, being overly critical, feeling a need to please, striving for perfection, and going along to get along. These are so typical and so ingrained that you may not recognize them as holding you back. It is critical that you guard against these patterns.

One of my favorite saboteurs shared by many of my clients, as well as my colleagues in the workplace, is "Yeah, but . . ." These two innocuous words, when paired together, can easily derail the best of intentions. After years in the corporate world, as well as meeting with hundreds of coaching clients, I can see this saboteur coming from a mile away. The first giveaway is the fidget. What is being said or proposed is both provocative and scary. They are excited about the prospect of venturing out of the commonplace that has inhabited their life. This is the "yeah." You can see their eyes light up with excitement. And then comes the look of concern, fear, and the fidget. It is as if a big cloud sweeps across them and casts doubt. People will begin to squirm in their chair, shuffle their papers, pull at their clothes, or play with their hair. Then comes the "but."

"Yeah, but" is something we adopt as we get older and pick up life experiences. Unfortunately, most of us have formed judgments and become conservative about what we believe is within our comfort zone and what is not. These two words keep us safe within our comfort zone but they also keep us from growing and evolving. "Yeah, but" is survival mode. "Yeah, let's give it a try" is thriving mode.

I was working with a lovely woman who really, truly wanted to move forward but was as stuck as if she were wearing lead shoes. Years of feeling frustrated about her living situation, coupled with a tough boss at work, left her feeling disempowered. She was suffering from "Yeah, but" in a big way. While she could articulate a core belief system that energized her, she was feeling unable to put it into motion because of this formidable saboteur. It would rear its ugly head whenever she was asked to step outside her comfort zone or activate one of her goals. With each prod from me, I would hear, "Yeah, but . . ." She is very bright and articulate, so she was extremely agile at convincing herself why she could not take action.

Well, the time came for me, the coach, to institute some tough love. I had to declare our coaching sessions a "Yeah, but"–free zone. Those two words were to no longer be spoken while we were working together. This was not easy, to say the least. In fact, I could see her with great intensity resisting the urge to say them. "Yeah, but" is quite forceful and persistent, especially since it is prevalent in so many places we frequent. One way to break down this saboteur is to replace the language. "Yeah" can stay, but the "but" needs to be replaced. It is pretty easy to do; use words like "I will give it a try" or "I can do that" or "Yeah, and." Making this change does require vigilance, but once people become aware of the "Yeah, but," they begin to see how disruptive it can be to advancing change in their life.

Exercise: Knowing Your Saboteurs

Now it is time to get intimate with your saboteurs. Write a description about your saboteurs. Who are they? What are they protecting you from? When are they the loudest? What are they telling you not to do? What do you feel physically when they are present?

When you are finished writing, read your story out loud. What do you think? How much validity do your saboteurs have? Are they really that powerful and intimidating? Or are they pretty tame, something you can manage?

Most of my clients realize their saboteurs are pretty pedestrian. In fact, when they see them written on paper and hear them spoken, they feel more in control of them and empowered to not let them take over their lives. For those who feel overwhelmed by their saboteurs, I suggest they seek the help of a therapist, who is better suited to help uncover deeper latent emotions.

Now, what are you going to do when your saboteurs show up? Here are some tips. You can just ignore them—pretend they don't exist and move forward like a wrecking ball against an abandoned building. You can acknowledge them, realize what they are trying to do, and tell yourself that they will not hold you back. You can speak to them and tell them they will not get in your way. You can divert your attention by focusing on your core belief system and what is important to you. Or you can just take a break from whatever you are doing and go for a quiet walk while taking long, deep breaths.

It Is About You

For most people, living their life doing the "right" thing means they have sacrificed what they want. Doing for others has become the norm. People rely on them and expect them to continue their previous behavior of always filling in. This is where many people get tripped up. They believe if they focus on themselves they are being self-centered. There is guilt, especially for those with demanding careers that keep them away from the family, or those whose income is the source of the family's prosperity. With so much economic uncertainty, people are paralyzed. "How can I think about me when I have responsibilities?" These two are not mutually exclusive. In fact, they are inextricably linked. If you are so focused on doing all the "right" things for others, you are probably not taking care of yourself. This may result in not eating properly or forgoing exercise, which will eventually break you down.

I see this so often with my clients. People's saboteurs misguide them by placing all their focus on others. This can be at home as well as at work. Unfortunately, some people will take advantage of your emotional generosity. All of us have limited amounts of time and emotional energy. They are finite resources. The more we give away to others who do not return it, the less we have for ourselves. What I want for you is to find the balance. This is the time when it is just as important to do for you as it is to do for others. I am granting you permission to be selfish with some of your time. I am also encouraging you to bring others along into your journey.

Reset Your Health: A Healthy Mind Needs a Healthy Body

To keep the body in good health is a duty . . .
otherwise we shall not be able to keep our mind strong and clear.
—BUDDHA

What's the state of your physical health? Do you have the physical energy to live to your core belief system and to actualize your Dynamic Goals? Are you beleaguered with health issues? Is your body riddled with aches and pains? While this book is primarily focused on how to help you get mentally and emotionally fit to change the arc of your life, you will also need to be physically fit. You will need a strong, healthy body.

The facts are unfortunate but true: Our bodies begin to break down in our forties. Our bodies suffer from the natural wear and tear of use and, in some cases, abuse. When we are in our twenties, living life as a free agent, our bodies are resilient and can withstand bad eating habits, lack of sleep, and indulging in excesses such as alcohol. Over time, the cumulative effect is that our bodies are no longer strong enough to fight back on their own. Therefore, ensuing health issues begin to take hold. According to the Centers for Disease Control and Prevention (2009–2010), the percentage of adults twenty and over suffering from chronic health issues is staggering: obesity, 35.9 percent; overweight, 69.2 percent; diabetes, 12 percent; high cholesterol, 27.9 percent; and high blood pressure, 46.7 percent.[4] There is no measure for fatigue, but I would guess it's very high as well. Most people think our bodies are invincible. We assume our bodies will withstand the daily rigors of life until we are old and presumably retired. But that is a fallacy. Not only do we face a mental and emotional arc in our life, but we are also combating a physical arc. Our bodies will naturally begin to break down and inhibit us from charging forward.

I became acutely aware of this fact while I was writing this book. By all accounts, I have always taken good care of myself. I exercise on a regular basis and eat healthy foods. This has been very consistent since graduating from college. I'm a regular at the gym; I play tennis and run three miles twice a week. I believe in keeping my body lean and strong. Knowing that as I age I could lose muscle and gain an enlarged midsection, I have ensured my workouts continue to incorporate both strength training and cardio.

Given my family history of heart disease and diabetes, I became watchful of what I eat. For many years, I was the guy eating salads for lunch instead of a burger and fries. I kept an eye on the latest in healthy eating and would incorporate the suggested foods that were heart healthy and could reduce cholesterol. In doing so, I vastly reduced the amount of packaged or prepared foods that I eat.

All was good until I started getting migraines and feeling fatigued. My mother suffered from migraines that were debilitating. It was not uncommon for her to be sick for days. This was new to me, however, and I didn't like it one bit. I began by reading as much as I could about migraines to understand the root cause. Why now? What was different? I started to document when they came and what I was doing. Were they stress related? Were they sinus related or from allergies? Were they from eyestrain? I was on a quest to diagnose and treat. Unfortunately, this went on for years with no relief in sight.

Accompanying my migraines was fatigue. Each morning it was a struggle to get out of bed, and I was suffering from energy dips throughout the day. In particular, during midday and early evening, I would find myself needing to take a nap. I was resorting to increased amounts of caffeine, hoping it would power me through the day. I was able to function well enough in order to get work done and meet the demands of my career and life. The trouble was that it was taking so much out of me that I couldn't muster enough energy to do more than what was expected. This is not a great situation to be in when you are starting your own business and your most valued resource is you.

At first, I thought it was stress related. I had recently left the confines of corporate life to start my own executive coaching practice. While I wasn't feeling any undue financial stress, it's always present whether you are working on your own or not. My health situation was troubling because I couldn't see this as part of my future life. There were too many things I wanted to do and being sidelined with migraines and fatigue was problematic.

One afternoon, I was having lunch with a friend. As I was explaining my situation, she spoke of a book she was reading that linked certain foods to inflammation and how inflammation can exacerbate certain preexisting medical conditions. As she was talking, I was buying it, hook, line, and sinker. It immediately made sense. When something resonates with me that deeply, I know that I have to take action quickly. Later that afternoon, I downloaded the book and read it in one sitting. It just clicked.

What you have to know is that I am not one to follow a diet, cleanse, or eating program. Only once had I purchased and followed such a program. I believed that if I stuck to whole foods—fruits, vegetables, poultry, and fish—that I would be okay. I was also eating copious amounts of supposedly cholesterol-reducing foods like oats, salmon, soy, black beans, and turkey. These foods were showing up in more and more recipes that were deemed healthy. However, this was refuted in the book, especially for people over forty. Many of the so-called superfoods were super bad if your body could not process them. At that point, I was really concerned since my diet was heavily skewed toward these foods, especially during the past few years—about the same time I was afflicted with migraines and fatigue. Could it be my so-called healthy eating was doing more harm to my body than good? I was both troubled and heartened because I thought I might be on my way to solving this mystery.

I began with a three-day cleanse to detox my body and create a clean slate where I could test foods to see what I reacted to. One thing I liked about the cleanse was that I ate real food. Throughout the three days, I was never hungry and felt satisfied. It was not all smooth sailing, however. During the second day, I had serious caffeine withdrawal headaches and felt like crap. My body was in full-on detox mode. Emotionally, I was pissed. All I kept thinking was, "I don't need this, I was doing just fine." Still, I persevered through this horrendous second day to wake on day three feeling refreshed, energized, and clear-headed. The cleanse was really working. I had a fantastic, productive day. It felt like some sci-fi movie where your body is scanned to eliminate all the bad.

After three days, I lost seven pounds, an unintended consequence. Losing weight was not my motivation. In fact, I had been at the same weight for so many years that I thought that was where I should be. Again,

I was wrong. The best weight for my body was seven pounds lighter than I had been. I spent the next seventeen days testing foods to see what my body reacts to. I've discarded most of the so-called superfoods in favor of more friendly foods. It was enlightening to go through this process. I now have a firm handle on what foods work best for my body. I can quickly tell when I eat foods that aren't good for me. For example, potatoes are a reactive food. This was shocking. How could something as innocuous as a potato cause that much damage? Well, it does, and I know it pretty darn quick. I also learned that canned and jarred tomato sauce, salsa, and soup are dangerous for me due to the citric acid along with the acid from the tomatoes. These had been staples in my diet.

As I was looking at my list of foods to keep and those to stop eating, I was initially disheartened, but that dissipated when I noticed how great I was feeling. My migraines vanished, and my energy levels surpassed where they had been before. I feel lighter and happier. My new weight fits me like a glove. I no longer feel bloated after eating certain meals. And if I do happen to eat foods that are reactive to my body, I know exactly what I need to eat in order to retain equilibrium.

There has been another surprising revelation: I feel more satisfied when I eat foods that are best for my body. My portion sizes are smaller, and the food carries me throughout the day without my ever feeling famished. It has been surprisingly easy to realign my eating. I make more mindful decisions when I eat out, without feeling left out. My new eating plan does eliminate a good chunk of the menu, but usually there are a number of options for me. Most restaurants will accommodate substitutions.

This idea of feeling satisfied is very intriguing to me. The more my food choices are aligned with what works for my body, the more satisfied

I feel. What did disappear are cravings. I am no longer craving foods, especially sweets. And when I do indulge in dessert, I only need a small taste.

I found that changing how I fuel my body makes for better workouts. First, I feel lighter, especially when I'm running or playing tennis. In the past, I felt a heaviness in my legs. Second, I am able to maintain my intensity longer. Previously, I would begin to feel sluggish halfway through my workout. And third, my recuperation time between workouts has decreased. I offer no scientific explanation for this change. Could be mental. Could be physical. What I do know is that when my body feels fresh, my mind responds accordingly.

My healthy body has also had an impact on my work. Now that I feel better, I have experienced a readiness to take on more clients and challenges that six months ago would have seemed too taxing. When my body felt lethargic, so did my mind. Always present was a negotiation between what I wanted to do (my aspirations) and what I had the actual energy to do. Now, there is harmony between the two. I know that with each commitment I make, I will have the capacity to deliver and hopefully exceed expectations. I no longer have a cloud of doubt following me, wondering where I would have a crippling migraine or whether I would have the stamina to meet the demands and rigors of having a successful, dynamic business.

People have been quick to notice that I look leaner and my skin looks healthier. Some have even gone as far as to say that I look younger. This is the second time that after undertaking a significant change in my life people noticed. The first happened when I took control of my life by living to my core belief system, and the second occurred when I took control of my health to eat foods best suited for my body. It's pretty amazing to me when people can see the difference, because in each case,

I would say it's been a subtle refinement, not a wholesale change. Therein lies the lesson: Sometimes a matter of degrees can have a noticeable positive impact.

I have highlighted the concept of control. *Control* can be a loaded word. When taken to an extreme, it can be dangerous and dogmatic. I believe that having control in how we live our lives is essential. Once I took control of my career, I actually made myself more open to opportunities. I built strong relationships that were mutually beneficial. I found myself more collaborative. And in all cases, I was moving forward on the vision I have for my life. Once I took control of the foods I eat and the impact they have on my body, I felt less likely to inadvertently damage myself. There are so many things that are beyond our control and that we have to accept. That is the undeniable reality. However, I'll do whatever is within my control to give myself the greatest advantage, and that includes taking care of my body and my health.

Fits and Starts

Creating a world in which you thrive is a process. Your arc will not soar upward in a linear fashion. It will have periods of highs and lows. You will start fast with initial progress, followed by fits of frustration that will require you to stay committed as you work through them in order to get another shot of energy. You know you are managing your saboteurs when you successfully navigate your way through your first low period. This can be the most challenging. You will be tested.

People experience this when they take on any goal that is challenging or outside what they usually do. Typical challenges include dieting, exercising, and tackling the big daddy of them all, *What do I want to do with my life?* It is not uncommon to have a dark, discouraging period when easy progress has halted, and to continue forward requires grit and determination. This is when fortitude and true commitment will push you over the finish line.

Here are a few tips to help you manage those dark periods of time when you are questioning your ability to thrive.

1. Know that it will pass. These are normal feelings; allow yourself to experience them but know it's only temporary.
2. Take a break and do something you enjoy, such as a creative outlet or spending time with your friends and family.
3. Do something that makes you laugh. Laughing is the perfect antidote when you are feeling discouraged.
4. Clear your mind. Write down exactly what you are feeling and why. This will help you isolate the real issues. It's less daunting to take action once you see them on paper.

Are You Suffering from Pre-Worrying?

A past colleague of mine shared a new definition of the word F.E.A.R.— Future Events Aren't Real. Wow, how true is that? I've come to notice many of my clients, colleagues, and friends suffer from pre-worrying. Pre-worrying is the incessant focus on events, situations, or conversations that may or may not happen in the future. These are scenarios that people have created but have no basis in reality. How much time do you spend fixated on fictitious future events? I am amazed at how creative we can be when we get into pre-worrying mode. We will play out situations and dialogue that we imagine taking place. Pre-worrying takes us out of the present and puts us into the future, thereby costing us precious time and the opportunity to impact what we can, which is the here and now.

I worked with a client who was ready to embark on an incredible journey that meant she would be faced with increased responsibility, heavier demands on her time, and a new partnership. This created an incredible amount of consternation. She was feeling very weighed down by the pressure. Her brain was in hyperdrive, playing out all the different scenarios and discussions that may or may not take place. In particular, she was concerned that with the increased demands she would not be able to deliver the highest-quality product that she had been known for and expected from herself. She was becoming paralyzed by future events that weren't real—the "what ifs"—so much so she was neglecting the here and now. And the here and now is where she can have the greatest impact. So we talked about her concerns. We looked at the future projects and the demands and assessed which ones were most important and required the greatest amount of attention and effort, and which ones did not merit as much attention. We also discussed some of the impending conversations and what she wanted to get out of them. In the end, she had a plan that focused on her desired outcomes and what she was going to do to achieve them.

Part of her plan included a visual metaphor for how she would respond when F.E.A.R. was dragging her down. She felt she was not able to get herself into a position of strength that would allow her to conquer all her projects. We talked about how she could shift her perspective to be in a more powerful position. For her, this meant sitting up high and seeing her surroundings. So, instead of feeling very weighed down by the pressure of the future, she now imagined herself riding atop a chariot where she had a view that was up high and expansive. She was no longer feeling dragged down. She had firm control of the reins and felt comfortable in how she was going to manage her newfound responsibilities and partnership.

The biggest impact, however, was that it brought her back to the present. She was able to move forward with her new projects with confidence and a game plan. She entered each uncomfortable conversation with a firm understanding of her desired outcomes, and because of that, she walked away with agreements that satisfied both parties. To this day, she references riding high atop the chariot, and while she is moving at top speed, she has a firm hand on the reins.

Why should you focus on desired outcomes when you enter a new situation rather than what could be? Four reasons. One, it forces you to crystallize and articulate what's most important and what's not. Two, you can't control what will happen, so obsessing about it is pointless. Three, you have better things to do in the here and now. And four, all that anxiety is bad for your health.

Anticipate Happiness

I met with this same client a few years later and she had the most spectacular insight. What would happen if we anticipated good things, more specifically, happiness? It is such a simple concept, and yet it's one we rarely entertain. We both sat for a few moments wondering what that would be like, especially for people who are dealing with the fear of aging. They see their youth as the height of their arc and the rest of their life on the downward slope, having to constantly manage the disappointments of age. How much would things change if they turned that notion on its head? What would our interactions with each other be like if we started every encounter by anticipating happiness?

Why is such an uncomplicated notion so difficult to put into action? There are two forces that are at odds with this concept. The first is our external environment. A big culprit is the office culture. For many, work has become a breeding ground for discontent. We may dread going to meetings with certain people because they are so negative. We are skittish about sharing our ideas for fear they will be ripped to shreds. We use language that mutes anything that may be positive. We are always waiting for the other shoe to drop. This way of being runs rampant in companies where there isn't a healthy enough culture to keep the behavior contained. And when we are immersed in it, we end up with this twisted belief that it is a badge of honor and duty to be miserable and find fault. How can anything good, productive, and sustainable come from such a despondent place?

And then we have our own crazy, mixed-up mind. This beautiful and powerful tool can play games with how we see the world. Not surprisingly, the more experiences we have, the more likely we will have disappointments. The more disappointments we have, the more likely we will get frustrated. Before we know it, all we begin to see is what's wrong. We become quick to criticize everything and everyone. Here's an example: I was having dinner with some friends one summer at a new restaurant. We were sitting outside having a great time, but one of my friends was beside herself because our waiter hadn't taken our drink order yet. There was no reason for such exasperation. We had been seated for no more than five minutes and she was already chiding our waiter. It felt like she was looking for disappointment and jumping on the earliest opportunity to complain. Our waiter couldn't have been more delightful, the food was really good, but it was hard to shake the bad vibe that was created at the outset.

Believe me, I am not a Pollyanna who only sees the good without acknowledging the bad. I know there is a time and place to be rigorous in thought and action. We need to have high standards. But it should come from a place of good. We should want our lives and work experiences to be pleasurable.

One afternoon, I went to a Starbucks. It was a particularly large, crowded store and my experience there had been hit or miss. But I went in anticipating happiness. I would get a nice coffee, rest my feet for a few minutes, and recharge my batteries. I got up to the counter, placed my order, and as I was pulling out my money, I heard, "That's okay, it's on me." My initial reaction was to ask, "Why? What's wrong?" I looked up and the barista had a big smile on her face. I said, "Thank you very much and have a great day." I added generously to the tip jar and moved along to await my drink. I was left wondering, did my anticipation of happiness set the stage for this random act of kindness? I do not know and will never really know, but I would like to think it played a part.

> *Happiness is not something ready made.*
> *It comes from your own actions.*
> —*DALAI LAMA XIV*

In the end, we can only control how we respond to any given situation. If you can focus on the desired outcome of a situation, that will guide you on how to respond. Shift your focus to the present where you can control what you are doing and how you are being. And finally, anticipate happiness and be open to what transpires.

KEY QUESTIONS

· How are you managing your saboteurs?
· What are you doing to take control of your health?
· What future events are you worried about?
· What are you doing today to anticipate happiness?

STEP FOUR

ADOPTING THE CHANGES
YOU DESIRE

CHAPTER EIGHT

REALIZING THE LIFE YOU WANT

One of the high points of my coaching is when clients reach their period of illumination, that moment when they can see the present and future with clarity and a renewed sense of vigor. It takes commitment and motivation to recognize it, live it, and see it through.

A Desire to Thrive

What thriving means to you is supremely personal and based on your core belief system. My belief is that thriving people move toward something that has meaning and resonance. When I saw my life beginning to come apart at the seams, I decided to move *toward* something rather than running away or allowing others around me to dictate my career. I took a stand on my own behalf to change the arc of my life. You can do the same.

Life is a long journey and we are not handed a map to serve as a guide. However, we do have our intuition. This valuable asset needs to be nourished and developed. Some people have such a strong inner belief they have learned to trust their gut from a very young age. Others who have challenged their inner belief in the past will question their intuition, especially when it comes to stepping outside their comfort zone.

Historically, I fell into the second group. I struggled with being really confident in what I wanted to do and taking the path that is filled with unknowns. Throughout my career, I had the nagging sense that I should be doing something more. I was plagued by a low-grade sense of restlessness. My mind and heart were never quite at peace with my career, and to some extent, my life decisions. This kept me alert enough not to be complacent; however, I was comfortable enough in my career and life to not feel compelled to take strong action. Therefore, I would make small adjustments to mitigate any really bad decisions but nothing substantive was gained.

In undergrad, I pursued a degree in accounting. Why? It is a tangible skill that would allow me to earn a living. During my junior year, I realized I had no love or even strong interest in accounting. I never had, but it seemed like the right path to be on. I did mitigate this bad decision by deciding not to become a certified public accountant, or CPA. All my classmates were going this route. You join a public accounting firm, slog through sixty-plus-hour weeks, and study for the CPA exam. The thought of it made me cringe. So I shifted a bit and decided to get a job in corporate accounting. This was a mundane job and it left me restless. In my quest to find something more fulfilling, I went as far as to call one of the other companies I had received an offer from to see if they still had openings. They didn't and I stayed on with my first job for four years. The truth is that I was able to quiet my restlessness by doing all the other things that one does in one's twenties, exploring one's decade of firsts. This was only a temporary solution.

Even then, I knew I wanted to have a greater impact on people. But I did not trust my gut enough to investigate it. I was afraid to veer off the path until a series of events left me no choice. I had to listen to my gut.

Looking back, the clues were always there. I had a desire to write and use it as a way to impact people. When I worked in advertising, I learned how to write for business. I did not take the time to learn long-form creative writing and use it as a way to connect with a broader audience. In 2008, I was selected to participate in a "leadership offsite" event for the top young talent, sponsored by the larger holding company that owned the agency where I worked. One of the exercises in the workbook was to answer the question, what do you want to be doing in five years? My answer: "Own my own company. Write something that will influence and impact people. Become financially independent. Never stop learning. Let go of control so others and myself can grow." When I got home from the offsite event, I put the workbook on my shelf and did not even look at it for more than four years. I pulled it out one day as I was combing through my books and flipped through the pages to find what I had written. I was shocked and surprised. I had not done most of the exercises, but this one was completed in detail. And now, five years later, I am living what I wrote. I have my own executive coaching practice. I write for my blog. I am becoming financially inde-pendent (this may take a while). I push myself to learn new things (this is especially challenging when I take on the impossible, such as learning French on my own). I have been doing all those things that I set out to do, without even realizing it.

What do you want the arc of your life to look like? How commit-ted are you to thriving in your life? I'm hoping you're going to answer "upward" and "very." But it isn't enough to simply answer the question and then say to yourself that you'll start later when you have time. I know this trick; I have used it myself. Being the dutiful coach that I am, I'm not going to let you off that easy. Therefore, I offer you seven steps to get you moving.

Seven Steps to Move You Forward

By focusing on these seven steps you will begin your movement forward as you endeavor to change the arc of your life.

1. **Take action now.** Start today by committing to make a change. Identify the one small step that can create forward movement toward that change. These small commitments can have a major impact on your life. Remember, the clock is ticking and time can be your greatest enemy. Get moving now.

2. **Take the time to write down your commitment.** The very act of writing your commitment down serves as a first and crucial step in thriving. This will make it feel real, and you will be more likely to make it happen.

3. **Craft your core belief system.** We all can benefit from being clear about what is most important to us—what we want our lives to be and what we must protect. Being more open and honest with yourself will serve as a guide for how you want to live your life and the impact you want to have on others.

4. **Listen to your inner voice.** Everyone has good inner voices along with the not so good, the saboteurs. The good ones are aligned with your core belief system and assist you to ensure you make decisions that support how you want to live. The not-so-good inner voices can detract from your thriving by reinforcing the idea that surviving is the best way to live. "You want to live by not doing anything terribly wrong. Do not rock the boat. You'll muck it up. You can live the life you want later!!!" This is the time to focus on the good inner voices and the possibilities.

5. **Set Dynamic Goals.** Establish a set of goals that are focused on

the short term (0–6 months), medium term (6–18 months), and long term (18–24 months). This will help you see where you are going and what you have to do to get there. There is also satisfaction in ticking off the accomplishments. These small steps will help you stay motivated.

6. **Enlist help.** If you are like me, asking for help is antithetical to how you operate. You may be thinking, "I do not need help. Asking for help is a sign of weakness. Not to mention the fact that I may not like what I hear." But given all you want to accomplish, it's time to throw that notion out the window. While it may not be easy for you at first, you will get better and will likely find that people are more than willing to help. All you have to do is put yourself out there and allow others to assist you. Let people know you need help, and quite often you will get the help you need.

7. **Forgive.** To move forward, you have to forgive others and, more important, yourself. We all have a long list of what we would have done differently. But the truth is, the past is just that: the past. While it played a role in where you are today, it is not an indicator of the future, especially if you have a commitment to thrive. Forgiving does mean acknowledging and coming to peace with the past. The release of this emotional energy will allow you to create space for the good you want to bring into your life.

Five Patterns of Behavior That May Thwart Your Plan

The journey to change your arc will be filled with periods of exuberance and unwavering commitment but also frustration and self-doubt. During the periods of frustration and self-doubt, you may begin to question yourself and fall into patterns of behavior that are counterproductive to moving forward. Unfortunately, these five common patterns of behavior easily thwart or prolong any attempt made to change. Raising awareness about these patterns will arm you with the fortitude needed to plow forward even when doubts are present.

1. Accepting the Status Quo (It Is What It Is)

Most of us are not real eager to grow, myself included. We try to be happy by staying in the status quo. But if we're not willing to be honest with ourselves about what we feel, we don't evolve.
—Olympia Dukakis

The voice of status quo says, "What's the use in making an effort? Nothing is going to change." You can trick yourself into thinking that history will just continue to repeat and the results will always be the same. Or you can feel sorry for yourself. "Oh, woe is me, I'm too old to make changes." But what is the nature of your status quo? Is your current situation the way it is because you've let life happen to you? When you let life happen, you passively respond to events in your life, either hoping that you'll catch a break or just solemnly accepting what is. History and the status quo don't have to dictate your future. You can change the status quo but you have to resist the temptation to believe that your past is a predictor of your future.

Remedy: Embrace an attitude that doesn't accept that you can't change. Believe in yourself and live in accordance with your core belief system.

2. The Cynic and the Sourpuss

It is very easy to get dragged down by the naysayers. They will create drama and obstacles as to why you cannot do something. This is especially true if it is something that will forward your life and have you realize and live your core beliefs. They instead will try to consume your time with a strong negative pull so that you divert your attention away from your goals and your mission. How can you focus on the positive and moving forward when others are chirping in your ear about their problems and sucking you into their trials and tribulations? This is where saboteurs have a field day.

Wallowing in the drama of others will suck all your positive energy. Your ability to move forward and create space for new behaviors will be determined by how you handle drama.

Remedy: Make a pledge to practice abstinence. Create a drama-free zone in your life. This starts by not engaging in the conversations that are about other people and have no good intentions. When people are spreading rumors or gossip, sit back and allow the conversation to wind down and shift to another topic. You don't have to make a big deal about your pledge to no drama, but if you cease to fuel the gossip fire, you will find the conversations will begin to wind down quicker or not ignite in the first place. It will be understood that you have no interest in these unproductive chitchats.

3. Feelings of Entitlement (This Is What I Deserve)

"I should be able to coast." "I paid my dues." "They owe me." It may be that you have made a lot of sacrifices for your career in the past. But given the competitive market and the pressure on the bottom line, you cannot assume you will get all that you think you deserve when you want it. I have witnessed senior-level executives face jarring reality either within their current company or when looking for a new job when their sense of entitlement was at odds with their situation.

This can be particularly true with new senior management where there is no history or long-standing relationships and camaraderie to lean on. If you have a new boss or management team, you are essentially starting from scratch. Depending on the goals and objectives of the new management, your responsibilities and how you operate are going to be questioned at some point. This may result in your feeling that certain new tasks being added to your plate are beneath you or that how you work is being challenged or that your decisions are being questioned. In the end, if you aren't prudent regarding your perceived entitlements, you may find yourself with the short end of the stick.

On the flip side, I often counsel people who are looking for a job. It's not easy looking for a job when you are in your forties. Common complaints are ageism, shifting skill sets, and salary caps. All of these exist and can be overcome. What strikes me is how often people don't help themselves. I have clients who will start a job search with a list of entitlements. They believe that they have earned certain "perks" that come with having put in time on the job. That may be all fine and good but that may not be what the current marketplace allows. Many people will begin the interview process by laying out what they need. What people don't realize is that you must first get potential employers interested in you and how you can benefit their company. Gain an understanding of their culture and how they work. If they don't offer flextime, you shouldn't make that a prerequisite for taking the job in your initial interviews. The perks you have from your last job may not all carry over to your new one.

Remedy: Sometimes we have to put aside our entitlements, especially as we enter new professional relationships. During the first six months of any new professional relationship or job you need to be on your best behavior. This is not the time to lay down your list of demands of what you will or won't do or how you will or won't work. If you have a new boss or management team, spend time getting to know what they want to accomplish and how you can help them. If you are starting a new job, do your homework while interviewing to ensure it is a good cultural fit. Ensure you like the people who will be your colleagues. Once you start to produce work that is the highest quality and take the time to get to know your colleagues, you may be able to get more of the perks you're accustomed to. You may not begin with all the entitlements you had, but new rewards and opportunities may be created.

4. It Doesn't Matter How I Look

Oh, yes, it does. How you look will determine how you are perceived and how you want to be treated. It takes only one-tenth of a second to make a first impression, and once it's formed, it's hard to change. One of the side effects of a time-challenged life or downward-trending arc is losing interest in how you look and present yourself to others. Whether we want to admit it or not, first impressions still rule within most developed countries. We judge based on what we see. Physical appearance significantly informs our judgments about others' personality and capability. Furthermore, one of the main reasons people are overlooked for a job is personal appearance. Not too long ago, people would take care in their appearance and how they presented themselves to others every day. If you watch TV shows from the sixties and seventies, you see people dressed up. Men usually had on a suit and tie, and women would wear a dress. People put forth an effort.

Even those who were not necessarily style mavens still put together a proper look. They had respect for how they looked.

I believe this also translates into your work ethic and the quality of the effort you put forth. If you are constantly in relaxed comfort mode, you may begin to get lazy in mind and action. The job market is too competitive for you not to pay attention to the details—including how you look. In fact, a careful appearance will probably separate you from other candidates. Making the effort to care for how you look should not only be core to your work persona but also integrated into your daily routine. You will look and feel better.

Remedy: Allow yourself a few extra minutes in the morning to iron your clothes, comb your hair, and put on makeup or tie a tie. Looking polished does not have to take long. When you first make this change, notice how others relate to you. You may find that simply by putting forth a cleaner, more manicured you, the people around you treat you a little differently. You can demonstrate your respect for yourself as well as your work by dressing with care.

5. Procrastination

> *Know the true value of time; snatch, seize, and enjoy every*
> *moment of it. No idleness, no laziness, no procrastination:*
> *never put off till tomorrow what you can do today.*
> —LORD CHESTERFIELD

Procrastination is probably the most problematic of the five patterns of behavior that can thwart your attempts at change. Procrastination has at its core three variables: time, information, and certainty. You may think you have plenty of time to take action. There is always tomorrow, until that turns into months, years, and even decades. In today's information-rich world, you can become paralyzed with the need to have as much data as possible to substantiate any and all decisions. And finally, the desire for certainty that what action you take will result in a favorable outcome forces you to constantly put off doing anything at all. Battling procrastination is particularly unnerving when you are acting of your own accord. Being proactive and forging a new path takes an incredible amount of inner drive and determination. Every day you have to steel yourself and your belief.

Remedy: Revisit your short-term Dynamic Goals and start taking action on one of them. Make an agreement with yourself about how much information you need to make a decision. You'll never know for certain how something will turn out, so trust your instincts and your heart and make the leap.

Effort Leads to Engagement

The extent to which we amplify our lives comes down to effort. I have noticed more and more people not wanting to make an effort. This is a subject with many layers. Making an effort and not achieving success equates to failure that can lead to embarrassment. Some people believe it is better not to have tried than to have tried and failed. Failures are more visible and real than not trying at all. That is a mind-set you have to change if you wish to thrive in your life.

Why should you put forth an effort if you do not know whether or not it will be a success? So many of us expect or want guarantees. If it isn't guaranteed, why bother? Instead of pushing ourselves and stretching our capabilities, we lull ourselves into complacency. Complacency is comfortable and safe. We become masters at doing just enough. Anything that becomes a real effort is too much. We rest on convenience. No effort means not caring. Not caring means settling.

Sophie's Story

Sophie was a midlevel manager with a technology company. After being in the same job for ten years, she felt stuck. Her attitude in the office varied depending on whether or not she felt valued by her team and her boss. At her best, she was thoughtful, thorough, and helpful. At her worst, she was dismissive, combative, and negative. Sophie's manager was her advocate and wanted her to succeed. She provided Sophie with clear goals along with constructive and timely feedback. Realizing that there may be something deeper, she also teamed Sophie up with a coach in an effort to determine what work would really energize and motivate her in the future. Sophie was willing to engage in the coaching until she was asked a very challenging question: "What do you want to do?" She couldn't answer. In actuality, she didn't want to answer. Why? "What if I state what I want and it doesn't happen? That would cause significant disappointment for me." There it was, raw, real, and uncensored. The security of not being disappointed was more potent than the possibility of success. In this case, the chance for success was pretty certain, since her boss was willing and able to help make it happen. It's not as if she had to do it all on her own. And yet, the "What if" was too strong a force for her to sweep aside. Sophie found it more acceptable to maintain a position of ambiguity about what she wanted than to take the risk on something new. ✍

Does this sound like a saboteur to you? It is! "What if . . ." is a very powerful and prevalent saboteur. It prevents you from fully engaging in your career and your life. It keeps you exactly where you are. Without challenging our "What ifs" we continue to live within a small box. There is a famous saying from Leo Burnett, the founder of the advertising agency I worked for: "Reach for the stars. You might not touch one, but you won't get a handful of mud either." This to me embodies effort and engagement. Exploring the "What ifs" may, in fact, open up possibilities that we never imagined.

All Sophie had to do was to have a conversation with her coach. She may have been able to come up with a job description that both met her needs and provided value to her company. In fact, her boss would have welcomed such creative and proactive thinking. Unfortunately, Sophie let this opportunity slip through her hands. I hope, in time, when she is ready, the same opportunity will present itself, and Sophie will take full advantage of discovering what she wants to do.

Sophie is not alone. People all over the country are forsaking full engagement for safety. If we as a culture ask ourselves why our economy has stopped growing we may realize one part of it is that we as people have stopped putting forth the effort. It takes effort to thrive. It also takes a willingness to fail and be vulnerable. New thinking and thought is generated by people who have the belief and courage to do something more.

- How engaged do you want to be in your life?
- What is your effort level at your job? At home? With your relationships? With your family?
- Do you actively think about what you are going to wear every day? Do you find yourself saying, "Why bother?"
- Do you spend your time with people who lift you up or bring you down?

When to Practice Patience

All this talk about procrastination raises an important issue. On this journey to change our life arc, when should we be charging ahead and when do we need to sit quietly and wait?

I work with a lot of people who are going through career transitions. Changing careers or changing companies is a process. For some, it can be a long process. And by *long*, I mean up to a year. When people are interviewing at a new company, it is probably the most important event happening in their life. Careers are very important to people. Their career consumes the majority of their waking hours. Career changes should be met with great care and diligence. More often these are hasty decisions because we want out of a bad and unpleasant situation. Once we decide we are ready to leave a company, we want it to happen immediately. We lose all our patience.

This is the typical pattern. As soon as a company shows interest based on your résumé, you become obsessed. You anxiously wait for the first interview. After the first interview, you bite your nails waiting to hear from the new company. The interviewer may have left you with a favorable assessment about how you did and the prospect of future employment. You send a follow-up email to remain top-of-mind and show interest. And then, you have to wait. "How long do I have to wait? It has been a couple of days. Why haven't I heard from them?" This is a thought pattern I hear a lot. Everyone wants immediate results. When we do not get them, we begin to disengage and doubt ourselves. Guess what? It takes time. In this case, the interviewee is absolutely fixated on getting this job. He wants an answer and he wants it now. On the other side, the people at the prospective company may be interested in the candidate, but they have a whole host of other tasks to do as well. They may have other people to interview. They may have to deal with an emergency request from senior management. One of the key decision makers may be out of the office. There may be a long list of reasons why they haven't immediately contacted you. Just because it is your number one priority doesn't make it the same for everyone else.

My patience was tested a lot during my career transition. There is one situation in particular I'd like to share. Three months after starting my coaching practice, a client asked me if I'd be interested in doing a segment for a local TV station. The segment focused on tips for finding a job in the New Year. I jumped at the chance. I was put in contact with someone at the TV station and we started conversations. I was totally jazzed about this opportunity. But after some back and forth, the opportunity fell through. The TV station said they would rather use me for a segment in May as part of a contest where someone would win career coaching from me. While I was extremely disappointed, I put my faith in the folks at the TV station and went about my business. I would check in every once in a while to say hello and share some tidbits about finding a job, just to stay on their radar, but I did not force the issue. May came and went and still no show. But I continued to be patient.

A few months later, the station followed through on the contest and called on me to participate. It was a four-segment series that ran in September. I was in three of the segments, including an in-studio final segment. It was great fun and excellent exposure for my new company.

This is a perfect example of why it is important to practice patience. I was initially crushed because I thought I had lost a great opportunity. Little did I know, the real opportunity was yet to come. Waiting nine months was slow torture, but I had faith that something better was on the horizon. If I had been impatient, getting upset with the television producer or no longer staying in touch, I could have blown the opportunity. After the first offer didn't turn out as I had planned, it would have been very easy to get discouraged or become vocal to the TV station about my disappointment. Instead, I decided to practice what I preach.

In the end, patience is a waiting game. The big question for most of us is "What do I do while I am waiting?" When we have our sights set on something, we are excited about it and it is tempting to let everything else fall by the wayside. This seems to be human nature. We put all our eggs in one basket. If it falls through, we are left empty-handed and we have to start all over again. Instead, the point when you have traction on an opportunity is when you need to push forward and look for more options. This applies to any time we are anxious to hear about a new prospect, and it is especially true when looking for a job. It is always better to have a couple of options to choose from. If you have interest from one company, chances are that you will have interest from another. When a company shows interest in you, you automatically feel good about yourself. It provides validation of your talents and value within your profession. That rise in your self-esteem will make you more attractive to others—the law of attraction. So now is the time to continue exploring other job opportunities. Now is *not* the time to take your foot off the pedal and coast, thinking you have the job.

The main reason people ease up if they have a good lead is that they are usually ready to move on from their current position. They have come to their wits' end and have already mentally checked out of their current job and company. This is typical behavior. I have been there. But this is when you have to really practice restraint. Continue to do your best work, and don't start telling people that you have found another position and are leaving as soon as possible. First of all, you have a commitment to your current employer. They are still paying you to do a job. Second, you will want to leave on a positive note. You never know when you might be knocking on their door again. I've been a returning employee. When I left my first agency the first time, I exited on good terms with a good reputation. When I wanted to come back almost eight years later, I still had some goodwill. Past colleagues were willing to support my return. There is a third reason as well, and this is important: *You do not have the job yet.* What if the company you are interviewing with decides to wait until next quarter to fill the job? Or they decide to go with an internal candidate? Or they just lost a major client and are not able to hire from the outside? There are so many variables that you can't control or anticipate. As hard as it may be, you have to resist the temptation to fantasize about your new job until it is a reality.

Learning patience is vital to making changes that will have the greatest impact. So, relax. Very few changes are going to happen immediately, so lower your expectations around timing. Finding a new job that is a good fit for you will likely take months, not weeks. It is a process, and many people are involved. You must also keep stoking the fire of opportunities. Make sure you have a couple of options. Continue to network and stay engaged in the process, even if you have a good lead. Nothing is final until the day you start. And finally, listen to your gut. If a company is really interested in you but you aren't quite feeling it, resist the urge to take the job in order to flee your current situation. If you take a job you know isn't right for you, you may end up in the same situation six months from now.

Some people's résumés are littered with two-year stints at various companies. Whenever I would interview a candidate with a résumé filled with short-lived jobs, I would wonder about their decision-making abilities. Some people career hop in order to continue to advance upward. If that is the case, you can expect them to leave after they have gotten what they could out of their experience with the company. Their mission is upward mobility. These folks are usually not team players and will make decisions based on whether or not something has value for them. Does it make them look good? Will they profit? Will they get some positive exposure? They will be a short-term employee lacking patience to see things through and weather any storm.

Mary's Story

Mary was very ambitious and had little patience for waiting to rise through the ranks. She was smart and knew how to quickly assess and leverage the politics of any situation. When starting a new job, she assimilated to the culture and cherry-picked her assignments. She was adept at pinpointing the right people to align with. Her focus was on her career trajectory and everything else was secondary. As soon as Mary felt that she had hit a plateau or others eclipsed her, she would move on to the next company. Her strong communication skills were very impressive and worked to her advantage when she was interviewing. She had a knack for engaging conversation and saying all the right things to seduce a new employer. Unfortunately, she never stayed anywhere long enough to build relationships and find real job satisfaction. ✧

Other people who have had a lot of short-lived jobs are fleeing a bad situation, so they take the first job they are offered. These folks are managing their career by minimizing bad experiences. Typically, they are not clear about what they want and are just happy to be out of their previous situation. Once they arrive, they realize the job is not what they expect or want. It is not unusual for them to begin plotting their exit.

Daniel's Story

Daniel was a competent employee but was not really sure what he wanted to do. He ended up in jobs by leveraging connections or being in the right place at the right time. He would start off well and then lose interest. Maybe the job was not what he thought: It was too boring, it was too stressful, or he didn't like his boss. As soon as the going got rough, Daniel got going. He was not known for putting in any effort to turn a situation around. Instead, he fled. First sign of trouble, and he started looking for the next gig. He got along with people, so he left a good impression and had lots of friends. His affable nature helped him land another job quickly. What it couldn't do was set him on a long-term path to thriving. His career suffered and his family had to constantly adjust to his new work situation. ❥

Neither Mary nor Daniel is on a sustainable career track. It takes a lot of effort to look for a new job and start over again and again. You run the risk of burnout and turning people off, and you deprive yourself of the opportunity to find an environment in which you can prosper. Adopting a core belief system to anchor and guide decisions objectively and employing a little patience in these situations will lead to a more conscious choice of career and a more rewarding job placement.

KEY QUESTIONS

· What are you going to start doing now to amplify your life?

· How will you defeat those patterns of behavior that could thwart your efforts for change?

· How can you make patience an active part of your life?

CHAPTER NINE

AMPLIFIERS: THIRTEEN THRIVING TIPS

Believe in what can be: Be relentless with your core belief system. If you do not have this, nothing will change. I never let go of my beliefs, even if it took years for the changes to happen and my vision to come closer to reality. I started making small changes that eventually began to build on each other. When I look back, I see great progress, but while I was in the middle of resetting my life, it felt as though everything was moving in slow motion. What kept me going was the positive impact I could see, even if in small increments. I also liberally used these thirteen tips throughout my life.

1. Manage Your Emotional Energy

Emotional energy is a scarce resource. How are you using yours? Focus it on what really matters rather than expending energy wastefully. I worked with a client who was suspicious of everyone. In her mind, no one was to be trusted. In many cases, it involved people with whom she had no relationship but had encountered tangentially. If a clerk rang something up incorrectly, everyone was out to cheat her. If someone cut in front of her while in line, everyone was trying to take advantage of her. If someone at the office questioned her work, they were out to sabotage her career. This consumed most of her energy and made her angry. The angrier she became, the more she would put herself on high alert, looking for injustices against her. The more bitter and disillusioned her view of the world, the more people began to pull away from her and her negative energy.

When you are younger, you have a higher tolerance for people who are negative. They tend to get buffered within a larger group of people. As you get older, your circle of friends becomes smaller, your life busier, and your stress level higher. After a while, you no longer want to be around those who drain your emotional energy. Who wants to go to dinner with someone who is constantly finding fault and casting a dark cloud over every situation?

It is essential for each and every one of us to manage our emotional energy. It is impossible to move forward if you can only see the bad. Letting go of everyday nuisances is the greatest daily gift you can give yourself. It takes a tad more effort to manage your emotional energy, but the cumulative effect at the end of the day is one of greatest happiness and contentment.

Try This: Focus your energy on the positive things that matter the most. Before you respond negatively to a situation ask yourself, "Is this really that important?" Your Dynamic Goals and core belief system will help you manage your emotional energy. Use them as a structure to assess how to react in any given situation.

2. Get Moving

Be active. Be engaged. Get off the couch and start doing. Nothing is going to change unless you put yourself into motion. Living a sedentary life can be intoxicating. Without awareness, you can spend most of your day sitting: in the car, at work, and at home. Exercise has not only physical benefits but also mental. It can provide a welcome relief from daily stresses and serve as a distraction from negative thoughts. Increased physical activity can lift your mood and improve sleep patterns. Exercise can also offer increased social contact by working out with a partner or taking group classes.

You can even exercise while working. Jeanie Caggiano, a senior creative director I worked with, installed a walking treadmill in her office—to be specific, her cube. Here is an excerpt from the interview I conducted with her for my blog.

Peter: What inspired you to buy a treadmill desk?

Jeanie: I read an article last year that said sitting more than six hours a day makes you 40 percent likelier to die within fifteen years than someone who sits less than three hours, even if you exercise. Well, most of my days are spent sitting in meetings. So the article made me think, but I didn't do anything about it. That all changed during a family visit, when I told my youngest sister, Neva, how great she was looking. She said it was because she'd gotten a treadmill desk and lost fifteen pounds. She works out of her house as a webmistress and easily spends her entire day on the computer. She'd read the same article, but did something about it—got a treadmill, mounted her monitor on the wall, put the keyboard on a slab of fiberboard, and started walking all day. My brother, Russ, who also works from home, went out the next week, bought a used treadmill, and fashioned his own desk. All around me it was happening, so I asked for one as a birthday present. I've been walking and working ever since.

Peter: Now you have me thinking about all the time I spend sitting at a desk. How do you use the treadmill desk?

Jeanie: Primarily for email and writing. It makes me feel like I'm not wasting time on mundane stuff like email. I also find the motion is helpful when I have to buckle down and write or concentrate on solving problems. I have found the best writing speed is 1.7 miles per hour.

Peter: It looks pretty tricked out. Tell me about your setup.

Jeanie: I had to attach my laptop to a large monitor so I can work at eye level. My keyboard is in front along with my phone and headphones. It's super convenient; everything I need is right there.

Peter: How much are you walking?

Jeanie: On average, an hour or two a day. I'm in meetings a lot. The most I've ever walked in one day was five hours.

Peter: Has it impacted how you feel?

Jeanie: While it has helped my posture, for me, it's been more psychological than physical. I like the fact that I am doing something good for me. It keeps me warm during the winter. And it makes me feel better about the time I spend sitting in meetings.

Peter: Maybe companies should outfit conference rooms with treadmills.

Jeanie: I've read that some companies have them available in common areas for people to use.

Peter: Any plans to have one at home?

Jeanie: Maybe. It sure would make paying the bills feel more productive.

After posting the blog, I heard from others who have done the same thing with their home office or have them at their place of employment. The takeaway is to build as much activity into your life as you can.

Try This: There are a number of easy ways to increase your physical activity. You can start by parking away from the store entrance and walking, taking the stairs instead of the elevator, and walking around your neighborhood. In fact, doing all three of these is a great practice. When you increase your activity during the day, you will find an improvement in your energy level and your attitude.

3. Lighten Your Load

Making change means making room for change. As we covered earlier, over the years, you collect a truckload of emotional burdens and responsibilities that weigh you down. By getting clear about your core belief system, you can shed emotional burdens that are not serving you well. This is a great start, but it is only half of the equation. Most of us have also collected sizeable amounts of physical items. We accumulate things. It has already been established that we are in a consuming economy that encourages us to buy, and we fully oblige. We have bigger houses with lots of space to store and keep stuff. Before we know it, closets become overrun with toys and gadgets, drawers are stuffed with clothes, and piles of papers begin to line the walls. Excessive amounts of clutter also weigh us down. As rooms become stuffed, the walls can easily begin to close in on us and we feel trapped. There is no room to move.

At some point, you have to begin to purge. My mother lived in our house for fifty-six years. As a Depression-era child she had a hard time letting go of stuff. Certain rooms became an open closet for all those things she was not using but couldn't throw out. The basement became a living archive of family artifacts but more notably a storage area for sewing material remnants, magazines from the seventies, wrapping paper and bows, not to mention outdated, broken tape recorders. This only scratches the surface. There were also empty cleaning bottles, unused hangers, and two sets of encyclopedias from the late sixties and early seventies. Keeping stuff that is no longer relevant does not serve a purpose. It is an action based in fear and will keep you in survival mode. Those who thrive know how to let go of the emotional and physical items that no longer serve a purpose.

When you begin to let go, you will feel lighter and less encumbered. Every year, between Christmas and New Year's, I clean out my closets and cupboards. The first year I did this was alarming. Unbeknownst to me, I was hoarding stuff like travel-size soaps and shampoos, expired canned goods, and papers—lots of papers. It was tough for me to throw stuff out, specifically those items that I thought I could use again. I was conditioned from a young age to keep stuff—even the broken, useless stuff—just in case it might come in handy someday. In truth, that day rarely if ever comes. So into the garbage it all went. Once I completed my first annual purge I immediately felt lighter and free from the clutter. I have yet to feel remorse for throwing something away. This is now part of my yearly tradition.

Try This: Pick a room in your house that needs to be decluttered. Create two piles of stuff, one to be thrown out and one to be donated. If you can't do it on your own, enlist a friend or family member to help. Once you're finished and the extra stuff is out of your house, ask yourself, "Do I feel lighter?"

4. Watch Your Time

Time is precious, and we can easily fritter it away. This is most alarmingly true when we are not under pressure. I found in business that people could snap into action when they were up against a wall and something serious was at stake. When I worked in advertising, I used to marvel at how quickly we could rally the troops when a client demanded better ideas or there was a threat to an account. This is true for any type of business when revenue and reputation are on the line. The true test of your inner drive is how you manage time when you are not under the gun. Self-motivation takes an impressive amount of inner drive and discipline few are born with. We all know those people who are incredibly focused and pack a lot into one day. The rest of us have to be extra vigilant about how we spend our time.

People often complain about how little time they have to make change in their life. But do you have a clear sense of how you spend your time? People who are becoming more mindful of what they eat commonly record everything they eat for one week. A twist on this is logging how you spend your time. For one week, write down what you do all day. With log in hand, you will have a clear sense of how you spend your time. Looking at your daily activities with a critical eye may shed some light on how you can find some of that elusive time. I have a guess that watching TV or surfing the Internet may account for a startling amount of time.

I'm sure you have heard the term *vegging out*. This is a common expression used to describe watching hours upon hours of mindless TV. Studies have shown that watching TV quickly sucks your energy. This passive form of mind-numbing activity is detrimental to your motivation. How often do you fall into the trap of sitting down to watch a few minutes of TV, and before you know it, hours have past? Or do you make it an evening ritual to hunker down on the sofa and watch a couple of hours of shows or on-demand movies? TV can be an intoxicating distraction after a long, stressful day. It was not uncommon for me to come home after a particularly challenging day at the office and escape in front of the TV. The times when this would reign supreme were when I was feeling unclear about my direction. I used TV to block out everything else. The problem was, I gave a lot of time to TV and got very little in return. Watching TV was not going to serve as a motivator for me to move forward.

I'm not saying to eliminate TV, but you should be aware of how much time you spend in front of the TV or doing any other passive form of entertainment and start replacing passive activities with active ones. Instead of three hours of TV in the evening, make it one hour and spend the other two doing something physical or something creative.

I'm a one-TV household and not too long ago it just stopped working. The cost to repair it would have been close to the price of a new one. This left me with no TV and a momentary sense of panic. While I don't watch a lot of TV, it is interwoven into my life. Before making a hasty decision, I did some research and finally settled on the one I wanted. The tricky part was that my TV is connected to a home theater system. That meant I needed someone to install and reconfigure the new set. The first possible install date was two weeks out. At first, I felt a little angst at not having a TV for that long. However, after a few days, I realized I didn't really miss it. I was having an equally enjoyable time doing other, more active pursuits. Eventually, the TV came and I liked having it for certain reasons, such as watching tennis; however, it's no longer that relevant in my life. I'd rather be up and active.

Try This: Sometimes it's hard to know where and how you spend your time. So for one week, keep a time journal. See for yourself where you are wasting time that could be put to better use. By cutting back on some of the more passive activities, you may find four or five extra hours in your week to spend on your goals.

5. Take One Thing at a Time

No more multitasking. It doesn't work. Only 2.5 percent of the population can effectively multitask, according to a 2010 paper released by Jason Watson and David Strayer at the University of Utah.[5] Many of you may be refuting this 2.5 percent, thinking that you have mastered the art. But Watson and Strayer are not alone in their findings. "When you perform multiple tasks that each require some channel of processing, conflicts will arise between the tasks and you are going to have to pick and choose which tasks you are going to focus on and devote a channel of processing to it," says David Meyer, PhD, a cognitive scientist at the University of Michigan[6]. That means multitasking may actually be slowing you down.

I've become keenly aware of how ineffective I am when I multitask. The test is when I do not remember what I just did, even simple tasks. This is particularly scary when I drive and talk on the phone (using Bluetooth). It is not unusual for me to finish my call and not know exactly where I am. Or if I have the TV on while I am reading, I find myself constantly rereading. My favorite is when I eat lunch while working. I will finish my meal and realize that I don't remember tasting what I ate. In fact, many times I do not feel satisfied because I am attempting to do too much. This is not good. Part of the multitasking problem is that too often we overcommit ourselves. It is time to slow down and enjoy one thing at a time. If necessary, take a few things off the schedule.

In reality, this problem is bigger than multitasking; it is about being engaged in what you do, and I mean *fully* engaged. People often complain about not feeling connected. Well, it is impossible to feel connected when you are only participating on a superficial level. And there is nothing worse than being on the opposite end of a conversation when someone is distracted. A few notable offenders are those who text while attempting to carry on a conversation, or type on their computer while on a phone call. Are you this distracted multitasking person? Here are some clues. You repeatedly ask, "Wait, what did you say?" or "I'm sorry, I didn't catch that," or "Huh?" Do you even look at the person who is speaking to you or are you gazing downward or over their shoulder?

I know when I'm on the receiving end in those situations, I will shut down and look to end the conversation. If this becomes a pattern with certain individuals, I find myself not wanting to spend time with them. If I am giving someone my attention, I expect the same in return. The concept is pretty simple: People want to feel recognized and heard. It is a gift you can give to anyone and it does not cost a thing. Think about how much better you feel after a meaningful conversation with someone. It can lift your spirits and make the other person feel appreciated. You are better off not conversing with someone if you are not able to be completely present.

Try This: For one day, do one thing at a time. Do you feel more engaged with each activity? How are people responding to you when you are fully attentive to them?

6. Consider the Company You Keep

I am not exactly sure why this happens, but as we get older, we have less tolerance for people who are not adding to our lives. This is a tricky tightrope to walk. On one hand, we do not want to become so insular that our view of the world narrows to only support our beliefs. On the other hand, we have less time and energy to spend with people who we feel are not enriching our lives. Put more crudely, the people who suck our energy have no place in our lives. I believe that when we are younger, we do not have the same level of awareness around who creates value in our lives and who does not. Yes, we have an idea of the types of people we like and will befriend, but we also have more tolerance for those who may rub us the wrong way. They may not align with our values or purpose, but we do not notice it as much.

When we become vigilant about the company we keep, we begin to make change in our lives. Going through change is daunting enough as it is, and you will want to ensure you have a solid positive network to promote your acceleration forward. That means having people who are in support of what you are doing, having people who will encourage you and aid in your journey. It means having people who can challenge your thinking in order to ensure you are covering all your bases. It means distancing yourself from those who are negative for negative's sake. These usually are the people who are disgruntled with their own lives and have no interest in seeing others succeed. Their mission in life is to keep others in the same muck they are in.

At work, you may have to adopt a high tolerance of others in order to work effectively as a team. This does not mean you have to spend social time with these people or even put energy into building personal relationships with them. To keep the naysayers at bay, you may need to set limits on how you spend your time with certain colleagues.

It can be hard to identify the naysayers and create the necessary distance when the negative people are close to you or are your family. To help, generate a list of people who are energy boosters and those who are energy drainers. Once you have the list, ask yourself why folks are on one list or the other. Then you can determine the role you want people to play in helping you move forward. It is hard enough to muster your own resolve to make change; the last thing you need is a naysayer who will keep you weighed down.

Most dyed-in-the-wool naysayers are scared of change and exposing themselves to failure. They definitely do not want someone else to step outside their comfort zone and be successful. For the naysayers, there is pride in ownership of being a victim. For them, there is a natural flow of reasons why they cannot move forward. They will be the first to tell you why you cannot move forward either. But what they really are doing is confirming for themselves why they are where they are. They are preserving their own ego and if you are not careful you will be pulled into their story of protecting the status quo. Mind you, this is usually not done with malicious intent, but the result can be very similar. So, accept them for who they are, but do not expect them to be standing on the sidelines cheering you on or offering a sympathetic ear during the dark hours of frustration and self-doubt.

Conversely, you will want to find your biggest advocates—those who will help you clear your path. Your advocates are people who you know love to help and support others in their success. More than likely, they themselves have found success by making change and moving toward a goal. You may have even admired them for their ability to take chances and step outside their comfort zone. These are the folks you want to align with as you move forward. They will have a good grasp of what it takes and will more than likely be able to help you activate your dreams and calm your fears.

Try This: Identify the people you admire or align with, and spend more time with them. What are their habits? How do they behave? How do they use their emotional energy? Do you feel better being in their presence?

7. Be Kind

I definitely maintain the belief that kindness toward others will translate to kindness in return. I want to say this up front: Being kind does not mean being taken for a fool. There are a lot of misperceptions around kindness. "If I am kind, I am a wimp." "If I am kind, people will take advantage of me." "If I am kind, I will never get ahead in business." I do not subscribe to any of those beliefs. To me, to be kind means to show respect and treat others with dignity no matter their economic class, race, or age. It is simple and it starts by acknowledging others. All too often, we get so caught up in our world that we cease to see others as anything other than an obstacle to be pushed out of the way.

Let's take an everyday example like the clerk at a grocery store, coffee shop, or gas station. I am mortified by the lack of use of the simplest form of a kind gesture, the five-letter word *hello*. All too often, I see people place their order, exchange money, and take their goods without uttering a word that acknowledges they just had an interaction with another human being. No wonder everyone is so pissy these days. We treat each other horribly. I am not sure why this has taken hold. Is it because we would rather check our smartphone? Is it because we are so busy and self-absorbed we cannot see anyone else? Is it because we have no manners?

I feel as though I shock store clerks when I say hello. Usually, I receive sincere gratitude from them in return. And it did not cost me anything. I also make it a point to say thank you with a smile when the transaction has been completed. To me, this is being kind. Nobody is taking advantage of me. I am not being a wimp nor is it affecting my ability to get ahead in business. But more importantly someone is feeling acknowledged and recognized for the effort he or she put forth. Think about yourself. How would you feel if throughout an entire day nobody recognized or acknowledged your presence? You go into the office and nobody says hello. You enter a meeting and the leader gets right to business and is barking orders. I can pretty much guarantee that you would not be feeling so great. In fact, you would probably be thinking, "What a jerk." And yet, how are you treating others? Bad behaviors beget bad behaviors.

Being kind may also mean putting someone else's needs ahead of yours. For example, you see someone struggling and you take the time to help him or her, even though it may disrupt your plans. This can be at work with a colleague or outside work with a complete stranger. There are no negative side effects. On the other hand, there is a boost of spirit after an exchange of kindness that will linger on and propel further positive emotions. I wonder what would happen if for a day, everyone showed kindness to everyone they came in contact with. Would the world have a collective smile and sense of being seen?

Try This: Make a pledge to show kindness starting today. This could be as simple as the use of "hello" and "thank you," a slight smile to a passerby on the street, or a helping hand to someone in need of assistance.

8. Meditate Nightly

I know that it is hard to control my mind. Left unchecked, it can be powerfully positive or it can send me down a rabbit hole. Usually, by the time I get to bed, my heading is spinning with the events of the day mixed in with the anticipated events of tomorrow. One day I realized that going to bed with this swirl of thoughts was making me restless and my sleep agitated. I decided to create short one-sentence meditations that I can read just prior to going to bed. The meditations address positive change I would like to make in three areas of my life. Not only do they help to remind me what changes I want to make in my life, but they also provide a basic system to reprogram my subconscious mind.

The sheer act of repeating these meditations that you want to instill in your subconscious creates a handy visualization. By repeating these words, you build mental images and scenes in your mind. The words help to provide focus on the desired outcome. Daily repetition makes the subconscious mind accept them.

You need to have your desires first, and the actions will follow. Often the two are out of sync, at least initially. You get excited about what you want and how you want to live your life, but the way forward is not visible. There may be too many options or none at all. In either case, you have to allow for internal processing time. Sometimes, the changes we want to implement happen quickly, and other times they may take months or even years. I believe our desires and actions align when we are ready. Staying vigilant to your goals and what you want is essential. I'm always amazed at what turns up for me when I'm ready to accept it. Along the way, it may be frustrating; however, as cliché as it may be to say, "in the end it works out for the best."

I know what you are thinking. Does this really make a difference?

Yes, this requires a leap of faith, but be realistic. Change is not going to happen overnight. But over time it will begin to take shape. Even if you do not buy into this 100 percent, you can at least acknowledge that saying the positive meditations just before going to sleep will end the day on a positive note.

Try This: Using a 3" × 5" card, write down a positive change you want to make in your life. How about another? And another? Each meditation should begin with "I am . . . " Read these three positive changes each night before going to sleep. Over time, do you feel different when you wake up? Are these changes seemingly more attainable?

9. Take Control of Your Spending Habits

"It's only . . . " is not reason enough to buy something. A big part of making change in your life is to take control of your choices, especially financial ones. Today's retail options provide a never-ending smorgasbord of products for anything and everything and at every price point. Specifically, there has been a steep rise in fast, cheap fashion and dollar stores. We live in a consumer-driven economy and I spent the better part of my professional career helping clients sell goods and services. I regularly find myself buying inexpensive stuff whether I really need it or not. I, like many people, suffer from the "It's only . . . " syndrome. At the time of purchase it doesn't seem like that big of an expense, so I don't give it much thought. But am I going to use it and do I really need it? Or is it something I will have to purge later? The point here is not to examine your detailed buying habits (although is some cases that may be necessary) but to take a closer look at your ability to manage your self-control. The more you take ownership and responsibility for your actions, the greater chance you will have of being able to live to your core belief system.

Self-control is also about self-management. This is about making the hard decisions and saying no when needed. Somewhere along the way, we decided it was essential to meet all our material needs and wants. That attitude usually shows up on our credit card bills. Credit card debt is at an all-time high, over $800 billion across the nation. This is a staggering figure. And it affects everyone at every socioeconomic level. Self-management requires you to become responsible and accountable. You may have to relearn how to make tough decisions. On a daily basis, I catch myself thinking, "It's only . . . " That is my cue to stop and really analyze the purchase. I find this to be especially true when I am clothes shopping during a sale. All too often, I will be swayed to purchase just on price. I routinely have to stop and really consider whether or not I will wear it. In fact, I will take it one step further and ask myself, "DO I LOVE IT?" That is the acid test because if I don't love it, regardless of the price, more than likely I am not going to wear it. It serves no purpose to have a piece of clothing hanging in my closet that I am not going to wear, even if the price was right.

The other culprits for me are discount or warehouse stores. Shopping the endless aisles, I am always likely to find something of interest for next to nothing. Before I know it, my cart is filled with "great deals." Individually, the prices are reasonable, so I can justify the purchase. But do I really need a thirty-six-piece set of plastic storage containers or a twenty-four-pack of T-shirts? I finally gave up my warehouse club membership and only shop discount stores when I have a specific list. No browsing for stuff. I feel more in control of my buying decisions.

We all can improve our ability to make decisions. This includes saying yes to the things that advance our ability to live to our core belief system and saying no to the things that are not creating more value in our lives.

Try This: For every purchase you make, ask yourself, "Do I really need this? Will this item enrich my life and help me live my core belief system?"

10. Employ Energy Motivators

Music. Cooking. Golf. To move ahead, not only do you need to have a belief system but you also need to know what activities give you joy. As your life has become consumed with doing all the "right" things, you may have lost sight of what activities make you happy. I have found that most people have traded in what makes them happy for what makes someone else happy. This is especially true for people who want to please others, seek a sense of belonging, or have taken on the role of caretaker to all. Being in service to others is noble. However, being in service to yourself is essential. To have the capacity to act with generosity, you need to ensure you are fully charged. You have more to give when you are feeling full and nourished. If you are always giving to others, at some point you will find yourself tapped out. This is when exhaustion and resentment can take root. Having a life filled with activities that nourish you is non-negotiable if you desire to thrive. This should not be confused with being selfish. You need energy to serve others as well as yourself.

What are your energy motivators? Think of those activities that make you feel rejuvenated and full when you are finished. These are the activities you want to increase in your life. Now ask yourself, "What do I need in order to create space for this activity?" Usually, it's something pretty simple. The hardest part is making it happen.

Try This: Write a list of five activities that give you energy. Which ones will give you the most energy? Starting with the most effective, write down how you can make this happen tomorrow. This sense of immediacy will put you into motion. Without immediacy, it will be put on the back burner and your energy level will remain low. Your task is to continually integrate those activities that will give you energy and keep you motivated with those activities that are in service of others but will deplete your natural resources.

11. Walk with Your Head Up and Your Eyes Open

There is a whole big, wonderful world out there waiting for you to be who you are and move toward your future. All too often, I see people with their head down powering through the day. I have to wonder, what are they missing? Well, I have a pretty good idea. I used to be one of those motoring through the day focused on the task at hand or the never-ending to-do list I had waiting for my attention. I was literally head-down and it was affecting my posture. I was hunching over and my shoulders were beginning to round. I did not initially see this, but after about ten people commented on my walking posture I took notice.

Posture affects how you perceive the world and how the world perceives you. To improve your posture, focus your eyes on an object in the distance that is at eye level or above. Make a conscious effort to keep your shoulders back. At first, you may feel as though you are fighting gravity and the natural pull of your body, but when you are vigilant about your posture, you very well may discover you feel better and your presence and confidence are enhanced. When I am overwhelmed with tasks, I find myself drifting back to my bad posture. This is my cue to stop running the list of tasks through my mind and come back to being present in the moment. I always start by lifting my head up and pushing my shoulders back. The tasks will wait until I am ready.

The other unfortunate by-product of keeping your head down is that you are missing out on what is happening around you. You are shutting down your curiosity muscle. Yes, I believe curiosity is a muscle, and if it is not used it will atrophy. Without curiosity, you will become one-dimensional and dull. Yes, I said it, *dull*. People who are not curious about what is happening around them or in the world are not keeping themselves fresh. They may think they know it all or have seen it all. Even on their daily routes, they have stopped being curious. They focus on getting from one place to the other. I am guilty as charged. I walked the same way to work for ten years. For most of those years, I would use my walk to work as the time to plan out my to-do list. I was oblivious to other people and my environment. My walk to work was turning into drudgery.

Around the same time I decided to address my posture, I also decided to open my eyes and get curious. Yes, I had walked the same walk thousands of times, but I was not seeing anything. I was dull. Now, I am amazed at how much I notice that I was oblivious to in the past. How morning light reflects off certain buildings. The construction details on the bridges. The relationship and scale between different buildings. The way people try to beat the lights in order to keep their pace. The flowers along the boulevard. Every day I see something I haven't seen before. I feel more engaged and aware of my surroundings.

This has the added benefit of altering your perspective. When your eyes are cast downward, it signals that you are not engaged. This is the mark of survival. You keep your head down and hope nobody sees you.

Remember in school, the teacher always called on the student who was head-down or looking away. People who are thriving have their head up because they do not want to miss anything. They are excited about life and want to take advantage of everything. The only way to take it all in is to be open. People who are open and engaged attract people. In order to thrive, you will need people around to help in your quest. Who are the people you are attracted to? When was the last time you thought, "Hey, look at the person with his head down, slumping along. I want to be his friend or business partner." My guess is not very often!

Try This: How about shifting gears for one week. Walk with your eyes up, shoulders back, and allow yourself to be curious about what you see and experience. Look for things that will bring a smile to your face. Take note of things you have not seen before, such as the color of a house, the signage of a restaurant, or the blueness of the sky.

This could be the beginning of how you bring more curiosity into your life. As adults, we have dulled our sense of curiosity in an effort to "get it all done." You will be doing yourself an incredible amount of good by restoring your childlike curiosity. In doing so, you will bring more enjoyment into your life and be open to new opportunities that you had not seen in the past.

12. Up Your Charismatic Quotient

One of the workshops I conduct teaches basic coaching skills for business professionals. I think people would be pleasantly surprised to learn that there is an unintended consequence of using basic coaching skills: They can make you more charismatic. Said another way, charismatic people employ simple, easy-to-use coaching techniques.

Charismatic people have the ability to make you feel better after a conversation than you did before. We all know these people, and we like to be in their presence. It is a skill that anyone can employ, and it starts with these simple tips and a genuine interest in someone else.

Try This:

- Listen more than you speak. And when you do speak, do it to ask engaging questions to learn more about the person and what he or she has to say. This makes people feel supported.
- Pay attention and respond not only to the spoken but also the unspoken, such as tone of voice or body language. This makes people feel not only heard but also recognized.
- Give people your undivided attention. Yes, that means no multitasking. You make eye contact, you nod, and you smile. Charismatic people make others feel like they are important.
- Be the first to pay someone else a compliment or acknowledge his or her achievement. This makes people feel valued.

13. Get Out of That Rut

Routines serve an exquisite purpose—to keep us on track and running efficiently. They are cultivated through years of knowing what we like or do not, the quickest way from point A to point B, and what will cause the least disturbance in our daily lives. Our routines become habits and guard us against repeating the same mistakes, squandering time, and having to re-create the wheel. We go about our lives eating the same foods, reading the same books, watching the same movies, and solving problems the same way.

When your routine is left unchecked, you are actively embracing a path of "sameness" and you become stale. You become so conditioned to your routine you see nothing else. Your life becomes smaller and your focus more narrow. And while you may find comfort in routine, you are also missing out. You stop discovering and exploring new thoughts, interests, and experiences.

For years, I would walk the quickest way to the office. This took me under the L tracks, where it's noisy and dirty. I became immune to it and accepted my walk to work as how I got from point A to point B. My pragmatic routine had become a rut. And then one day, I thought, "What if I walked along the river?" Yes, it takes a few minutes longer, but it's a completely new experience. There is a great view of the city, the river, and people. I'm more observant, and each day I notice something new. That was never the case when I walked under the L tracks. I was too busy negotiating around pigeons and crowds of commuters. Now, by the time I get to the office, I feel refreshed and energized.

Try This:

· Shock your palate. Eat a food you hated as a child. It may taste different now that you are an adult. For me, it was rediscovering Brussels sprouts (roasted).

· Spice up your lunch. Break bread with someone you wouldn't normally invite to lunch. Bonus points if it's someone you are at odds with. Get to know him or her as a person. Don't talk about work.

· Throw away the handbook. The next time you are confronted with a challenge, especially at work, resist the temptation to do as you always do. See it from a different perspective.

- Make a fool out of yourself. Do something that makes you feel uncomfortable, something at which you might fail. A few years ago, I sang two songs (badly) at a piano bar. It was not pretty, but I knew if I could do that, I could easily stand up in front of any group of people and talk.
- Seek out some adventure. Do something you've wanted to do but have not made the time for.

It's easy to become complacent during your forties and fifties. After being so outwardly focused in your twenties and thirties, you can easily slip into comfortable life patterns, feeling that you've already tried and experienced so much. In order to sustain a thriving life, you have to continually challenge your mind and body to stay fresh and engaged. We have to shake things up in order to know that we are still alive.

KEY QUESTIONS

- What are you being complacent about in your life?
- How are you going to shake it up?

PARTING WORDS

It's not the years in your life that count. It's the life in your years.
—A*BRAHAM* L*INCOLN*

When I set out to make changes in my life and live the life I wanted, I had no idea what would ensue. And to an extent, I still don't. But what I do know is that when I began my journey, I first had to interrogate my life before I could change my arc. There was no question that I wanted to move upward and onward. Clinging on and hoping for the best was not an option. I wrestled control and took accountability for my life and how I am going to live it. I needed a guide and inspiration. This is where formulating my core belief system became my invaluable asset.

Thanks to the effort I put into developing my core belief system, I have a vision for my life that serves as the foundation for how I am living. I have a purpose that shapes the impact I want to have on others. I have a set of values that guides how I live my life and the choices I make. The past five years have been exhilarating and nerve-wracking. I have embraced what I love doing and left the comforts and confines of a career that defined me for the better part of two decades. In that career, I achieved professional and financial success but felt constrained by the structure that was created around me. Many of these constraints were self-imposed and many were institutional. With the constraints lifted, I feel my creativity and drive have flourished; however, it is up to me to see it through. This is both a lift to my spirit as well as a constant reminder to stay focused on activating and amplifying my core belief system every day.

For me, my creativity took hold in the form of writing. While I spent twenty-five years honing my business writing skills, writing decks, conference reports, and pithy emails, I never permitted myself to pursue writing for a broader audience. But to support and build my business, I made a commitment to write a blog. This forced me to conquer my old foes and address each saboteur and insecurity on a weekly basis. To this day, I still have a tinge of anxiety when I hit "publish" and my new blog post goes live. But I know it is an expression of my core belief system and provides value to those seeking to thrive in their career, life, and health.

It is not always easy to live the life you want. It takes plenty of hard work. There is no phoning it in or just getting by. You have to take responsibility for life and the actions needed. This means facing your truths and making the decision to thrive. It entails having tough conversations whether with your employer or with those you love. In many cases, the result is redefining your relationship and your journey together. This book is a great example of hard work. For me, it was a daunting undertaking. On many occasions, I forced myself to sit at my desk and push through all my insecurities to keep writing and believing that exposing myself to vulnerability will create value for others. This is tough for someone who is more likely to undershare with others than overshare.

In retrospect, adopting change has not been the biggest challenge; staying open to evolving and growing has been even more demanding. Once I decided to become a coach, I was all in. While my vision and purpose have remained constant, how they manifest has been and is in constant evolution. That I did not expect. I assumed that I had a clear path forward. Boy, was I mistaken, and thankfully so. Originally, I planned to coach individuals only. But I realized that I still have a strong affinity for business and helping leaders be more effective in their role. This also carried over to helping teams work better together by understanding their culture and how to drive toward a vision. My inner actor also wanted some air time, so I created a coaching skills workshop that exposes business professionals to the merits of coaching skills in managing people, inspiring action, and creating strong customer service relationships. On a few occasions, I have been a career expert on TV, offering coaching to people looking for their next job. Many of these opportunities I had to seize and then trust my instincts.

The most rewarding aspect of the past five years is how much better I know myself and how accepting I am of my strengths and weaknesses. This deep self-awareness has allowed me to clear my path. I no longer pine for what I am not good at or wish I had but instead concentrate and embrace what I am good at. I feel liberated. In the past, I was so focused on doing the "right" things and being the "right" person that it was creating ongoing frustration and turmoil within my own being. Addressing the turmoil head-on means I am no longer beating myself up over what I am not. I am also focusing and articulating what I want and going after it. No more second-guessing (okay, maybe a little; I am human, after all).

Each person will figure out his or her midlife differently. However, following these four steps to amplify your career and life—interrogating your life, formulating a plan to amplify your life, conquering old foes, and adopting the changes you desire—serve as a blueprint from which you can map your future. And while you move onward and upward, your core belief system will be your guidepost for making decisions, lifting your spirits, and ensuring you stay focused on what matters most. My hope is that you believe in yourself and the notion that you have the capacity to change your arc and thrive.

NOTES

1   Kim Parker and Eileen Patten, "The Sandwich Generation," *Pew Research Social & Demographic Trends*, January 30, 2013, http://www.pewsocialtrends.org/2013/01/30/the-sandwich-generation/

2   Elizabeth Dias, "The TIME Creativity Poll," *Time*, April 26, 2013, http://business.time.com/2013/04/26/the-time-creativity-poll/slide/introduction/

3   American Psychological Association, "APA Survey Finds Feeling Valued at Work Linked to Well-Being and Performance," March 8, 2012, http://www.apa.org/news/press/releases/2012/03/well-being.aspx

4   Center for Disease Control and Prevention, (2009-2010) www.cdc.gov/nchs/fastas/

5   Jason Watson and David Strayer, "Supertaskers," *Psychonomic Bulletin & Review* 17, no.4 (August 2010): 479–85, http://link.springer.com/article/10.3758%2FPBR.17.4.479

6   J. S. Rubinstein, D. E. Meyer, and J. E. Evans, "Executive Control of Cognitive Processes in Task Switching," *Journal of Experimental Psychology* 27, no. 4 (August 2001): 763–97, http://www.ncbi.nlm.nih.gov/pubmed/11518143

FURTHER READING

**These books have beautiful insights that inspired me to
live a thriving life.**

- Harris, Dan. *10% Happier.* New York: It Books, 2014.

- Rubin, Gretchen. *The Happiness Project.* New York: Harper, 2009.

- Loehr, Jim. *The Power of Story.* New York: Free Press, 2007.

- Miedaner, Talane. *Coach Yourself to Success.* New York: McGraw Hill, 2000.

- Carson, Rick. *Taming Your Gremlins.* New York: HarperCollins, 2003.

- Sher, Barbara. *Wishcraft.* New York: Ballantine Books, 2009.

- Brown, Brene. *Daring Greatly.* New York: Penguin Group, 2012.

- Tolle, Eckhart. *The Power of Now.* Novato, CA: New World Library, 1999.

- Hollis, James. *Finding Meaning in the Second Half of Life.* New York:
  Penguin Group, 2006.

- Tharp, Twyla. *The Creative Habit.* New York: Simon & Schuster, 2003.

- Cain, Susan. *Quiet.* New York: Crown Publishers, 2012.

These books helped me change the way I eat and feel.

- Recitas, Lyn-Genet. *The Plan.* New York: Hachette Book Group, 2013.

- Davis, William. *Wheat Belly.* New York: Rodale, 2011.

These books have great practical tips.

- Rath, Tom. *Strengths Finder 2.0.* New York: Gallup Press, 2007.

· Edwards, Paul, and Sarah Edwards. *Finding Your Perfect Work*. New York: Putnam, 1996.

· Compendium. *Where Will You Be Five Years From Today?*

ABOUT THE AUTHOR

Peter C. Diamond "TheAmplifyGuy" is a professionally trained, certified coach who helps clients improve work performance and derive a greater level of career fulfillment. His ability to listen and guide clients to successfully determine the direction of their professional careers is based on his ability to initiate open, honest, and meaningful dialogue focus-  ing on the practical matters of career and leadership development.

Peter has been a business professional for over twenty-five years, with experience in marketing, advertising, and finance. Having distinguished himself as a recognized leader managing large teams, coaching individuals has always been front and center in his leadership philosophy. He places a premium on building highly functioning, cohesive teams that have a positive impact on the organization. Peter's satisfaction comes from coaching senior level executives one-on-one and coaching teams to help them develop to their full potential.

He started his private coaching practice in 2010, and in 2011 he was instrumental in developing and launching a full-scale executive and team coaching practice at Leo Burnett, where Peter now serves as an outside consultant. Other corporate clients include United Airlines, National

Association of Realtors, Razorfish, mcgarrybowen, Fresenius Kabi, PVS Chemicals, Human Rights Watch, and Intelligentsia Coffee.

Peter writes a weekly blog, *TheAmplifyGuy*, has appeared on ABC's *Windy City Live* and WGN's *News at 5*, and is available for speaking engagements.

He has an MBA from DePaul University and a BA from Michigan State University. Peter then became a certified professional co-active coach through the Coaches Training Institute. He is also a professional certified coach through the International Coaches Federation. Peter also received profile certification training (individuals and teams) from The Leadership Circle and completed the Organization and Relationship Systems at Work course through the Center for Right Relationships.

Additional Ways to Amplify

Visit www.petercdiamond.com.

Follow Peter's blog at petercdiamond.com/theamplifyguy.

Peter is available for speaking engagements, media opportunities, panel discussions, and workshops.

Peter can be reached at peter@petercdiamond.com.

READING GROUP GUIDE

1. How does the idea of Amplify Your Career and Life resonate with you? What's the author's intent with writing the book? What inspired you to read the book?

2. The author talks about the challenges of midlife, Do these feel relevant to you or others you know? Why or why not? What would you add to the list? Has the book provided a new perspective on the concept of midlife?

3. What is the state of your life arc? Is it on an upward swing or a downward slope? Is your career and life in flux? What have you been doing because it's the "right" thing to do? Where do you feel boxed in? How are you taking control of your life's arc?

4. The author uses other people's stories as well as his own to bring to life key concepts in the book. How does this help inform the story? Does it make the content more relatable?

5. What did you learn about yourself after completing your Life Line Assessment? How did that exercise inspire your Dynamic Goals? What actions are you taking to fulfill your goals? What support do you need from others?

6. Is the concept of a core belief system (vision, values, purpose) meaningful to you? Why or why not? How are you opening yourself up for change?

7. The author identified five universal themes that emerge as people begin to rediscover what's most important to living an amplified life. Which ones resonate with you the most?

8. What's holding you back from amplifying your career and life? Are you suffering from pre-worrying? How are you managing your saboteurs so they don't keep you from moving forward? Which of the five patterns of behavior are thwarting your plan?

9. What are you doing to anticipate happiness? Which amplifiers are you already putting into practice? What commitments are you making to yourself to uncover what's best about you and how to use it?

10. What have you noticed that's different about yourself and your outlook since reading the book?

Download the Amplify Your Career and Life Workbook at petercdiamond.com

CPSIA information can be obtained at www.ICGtesting.com
Printed in the USA
LVOW12s1948061014
407459LV00004B/5/P